I'LL BE DAMNED

I'LL BE DAMNED

HOW MY YOUNG AND RESTLESS LIFE LED ME TO AMERICA'S #1 DAYTIME DRAMA

ERIC BRAEDEN
WITH LINDSAY HARRISON

DEY ST.
An Imprint of WILLIAM MORROW

TO MY GRANDCHILDREN—
MAY I PASS ALONG TO YOU THE GOOD HEALTH,
THE LOVE OF LEARNING,
THE GIFT OF DREAMS
AND THE DRIVE TO MAKE THEM COME TRUE
THAT HAVE HELPED DEFINE MY LIFE.

All insert photographs courtesy of the author unless otherwise indicated.

Script in Chapter Eight, "The Young and the Restless" © 2016 CPT Holdings, Inc. Courtesy Sony Pictures Television.

Title page photograph © 2016 CPT Holdings, Inc.

HarperCollins books may be purchased for educational, business, or sales promotional use. For information, please e-mail the Special Markets Department at SPsales@harpercollins.com.

A hardcover edition of this book was published in 2017 by Dey Street Books, an imprint of William Morrow.

FIRST DEY STREET BOOKS PAPERBACK EDITION PUBLISHED 2017.

Designed by Renata De Oliveira

Library of Congress Cataloging-in-Publication Data has been applied for.

ISBN 978-0-06-247612-8

21 22 LSC 10 9 8 7 6 5 4

CONTENTS

FOREWORD BY STEPHEN A. SMITH, ESPN

I laughed when I first learned of the title, *I'll Be Damned*. Not just because of its appeal but also because of its authenticity. Because if you talk to Eric Braeden, if you listen to him, you walk away in the same fashion one imagines all those *Y&R* fans have walked away from their television sets all of these years: marveling at his greatness, his wisdom, his genuine kindness, and his humility. But, most importantly, his realness.

You get it all when you're in the presence of this man, filled with depth beyond his years and passion to boot, yet filled with the kind of authentic emotion capable of diminishing the apathetic or indifferent amongst us to shame.

Eric is a man who loves his native Germany yet recognizes elements of its shame. The same can be said when he talks about America, a nation he clearly loves but works tirelessly for, to help make better. He remembers the desolate amongst us because he recalls being one of them. He appreciates his fans because he remembers not having any. He speaks for the disenfranchised amongst us, understanding that a nation is no stronger than its weakest link. And he does so by reminding those willing to listen that there's simply no other way to be—because it is right . . . and just . . . and decent.

Eric Braeden is German. I am American. He is a white man; I am black. He is nearly twenty-five years older than I am—so you'll be hard-pressed to ever catch us partying together.

He also happens to be one of the greatest men I have ever had the pleasure of knowing, who has blessed me with a great friendship. One I fully anticipate will last until the day I die.

His wealth of knowledge is a gift in itself. His truth, shared through his personal stories and journey, is even better. When he speaks, we all should listen. Leaders—including presidents—have been advised by lesser men.

I'll Be Damned is a must read for any and all primarily because of its truth, coming from a man who knows of little else. It's about his journey. His world. His life. And how so many of us can benefit from what he conveys to us all.

I know I have already. I'd advise all of you to do the same.

You'll be better for it. And the best part is, knowing Eric, that's all he ever wants for anyone, anyways.

INTRODUCTION

It was a bright, warm day in southern California when I found myself being presented with a star on the Hollywood Walk of Fame, the first German-born actor since the legendary Marlene Dietrich to receive that honor.

My extraordinary, supportive wife Dale was there. My son Christian, the pride of my life, was there. My good friends Mike Meyer and Jürgen Janson were there. George Kennedy was there, that iconic bear of a man who'd co-starred with everyone from John Wayne to Cary Grant to Paul Newman and won an Oscar in the process. Jesse Ventura, former professional wrestler and Minnesota governor, spent a few moments at the microphone. Boxing great Kenny Norton was there, as was Los Angeles city councilman Tom LaBonge. The press was there, along with a large crowd of cheering fans. And last but certainly not least, my castmates from *The Young and the Restless* were there, right by my side where they belonged, appropriately sharing a spotlight I knew I owed to that show and to every one of them.

It was one of the most overwhelming, surreal, humbling moments of my life as I knelt beside that star with my name on it, in the heart of Hollywood, and scanned the faces of so many people I loved. It was impossible to take it all in and impossible to keep my mind from wandering back to the journey that brought me there . . .

The *Young and the Restless* contract I'd been reluctant to sign because I wasn't sure I wanted to commit to playing this Victor Newman character for the three long months they were offering . . .

The amazing global travel and acclaim *Y&R* had afforded me . . .

The decades of television, film, and theater work that started with such mystified awkwardness . . .

The years of parking cars and moving furniture to keep a roof over my head . . .

The once-in-a-lifetime adventure that brought me to Los Angeles in the first place . . .

Coming to America, making my way as best I could in a strange land with no money, no sense of direction, no idea what I wanted to do with my life, cutting up cadavers, working as a ranch hand, freezing in a lumber mill while I tried to figure it out . . .

And the little German town, scarred by the cruel bombs of World War II, where my life began and took shape, where I first learned about privilege and poverty and love and loss and sports and hard work, where I would never have allowed myself to even dream of a day like today, let alone imagine it might actually come true.

A star on the Hollywood Walk of Fame. I'll be damned.

1

BEGINNINGS AND ENDINGS

I can't imagine my mother's fear on the night I was born.

It was April 3, 1941. She and two hundred other women, all waiting to give birth, were gathered in the dark, airless basement of a hospital in Kiel, Germany. Bombs from the Allied forces of World War II thundered around them, sirens screamed, the ground shook with one explosion after another, and she must have felt so alone and so terrified as she lay there praying for the safe delivery of her child.

I arrived just in time. A few days later, another swarm of bombs destroyed the hospital where I took my first breath.

I was named Hans Jörg Gudegast, the third of four boys

born to remarkable parents who did their best to give us as normal a childhood as possible in the midst of that war's unspeakable obscenities. Kiel was a port city, and because submarines and warships were built there, it was a popular target for the Allies, as was Hamburg, seventy miles away. In fact, by the time the war was over, some five hundred thousand bombs had been dropped day and night in Kiel alone, five hundred thousand bombs that destroyed 96 percent of a city where good people and innocent children lived.

I was four years old when World War II ended. My memories of it come in brief flashes that still haunt me—deafening explosions and massive fires that lit up the countryside . . . our parents frantically carrying us to the basement at the first roar of approaching Allied bomber squadrons . . . burning farms and helpless screaming animals in flames . . . my teenage brother hoisting me onto his shoulders to see the city of Hamburg transformed into an inferno by firebombs that killed tens of thousands of civilians in one night . . . thousands of homeless, hungry people descending desperately on the farmlands around our village to dig for potatoes and kernels of wheat . . .

As a little boy, with nothing to compare them to, I wonder if I thought those horrors were normal, that they were simply part of what everyday life was like in this world.

I was among the lucky ones for whom everyday life was happy for many years after the war ended. That nightmare had left plenty of devastation in its wake—many neighboring farms lay decimated, and some of our teachers had returned from the Russian front with no legs or one arm and great bitterness. But my brothers and I quickly discovered that those farms and the rest of the countryside were wonderful places for four strong, healthy boys to work and play, that we happened to live in a big, beautiful house with three maids and two drivers, and that we were blessed with two extraordinary parents who loved us very much.

Mother was a strong, proud, affectionate woman, a member of the landed gentry who, I was told later, was thought by her family to have married below her class when she and my father found each other. She loved to laugh, and she had, and needed, limitless energy with four sons. She always made sure we presented ourselves well, especially in church, where we delighted in making her giggle against her will during the sermon, and on our Sunday afternoon walks through the village of Bredenbek, on the outskirts of Kiel, with our father, the local mayor.

I was very close to my father. He was a man's man, warm and funny and highly respected. Although he only spanked me once, when I was caught smoking behind the house at eleven years old, all it took was a look and a stern, simple, "Boys . . . ?" from him and the four of us would instantly stop whatever misbehavior we were up to. He hosted frequent dinner parties at our house, sitting at the head of a table filled with his family and local dignitaries. I was notorious for hiding behind whatever dignitary I was seated beside and making faces so that I could watch everyone else at the table struggle not to laugh, and I could always hear a subtle amusement in his voice when my father scolded me for it after the guests went home. He had a gift with his sons, no matter how angry he was with us or how much we deserved it, of never making us feel disrespected by him, or less than adored.

My brothers and I fought with each other as enthusiastically as we played, of course, and no fights were more predictable than those involving which of us was going to drive our father's car without his knowledge while he took care of business around town. He would take us with him on errands and disappear into some office or store, the fighting would begin, and within moments the winner would be behind the wheel, chauffeuring his brothers on a brief tour of the immediate vicinity and then parking and hurriedly switching seats again before our father emerged and drove on to his next stop. It was thanks to those excursions that I learned to drive when I was nine or ten years old, still small enough that the top of my head barely reached the bottom of the car windows, so that on at least one occasion my mother was treated to the sight of our car cruising down the street apparently driving itself.

Like so many Germans, my father had to start over from nothing at the end of the First World War. He was a farmer when the Nazi era began, and he was asked to loan out some of his farm equipment to build roads, which evolved into buying trucks to lease, which evolved into starting a construction business and moving his growing family into the village of Bredenbek, where he was elected mayor. He was a smart, honest, successful man, and like most German professionals in the early 1930s, he joined the Nazi Party.

The unspeakable atrocities that Adolf Hitler and his henchmen inflicted too often tend to overshadow the story of Hitler's rise to power. There seems to be a common, insane assumption that one day in 1933 he stepped up to a microphone and announced, "I'm a racist, anti-Semitic, power-crazed monster who intends to eradicate all Jews and anyone who disagrees with me," and Germany cheered and embraced him as their new chancellor. Like most sociopaths, Hitler was much more seductive and insidious than that, and neither my father nor my country nor any human being with connected brain cells and a conscience would have tolerated him for a moment if he'd been honest about his intentions.

Germany was severely weakened by World War I. Then came the punitive Treaty of Versailles, drafted in 1919 by the Allied forces, which contained a clause demanding that "Germany accept the responsibility of Germany and her allies for causing all the loss and damage" during the war—a clause written with the intention of making it economically impossible for the Germans to start another war. The American stock-market crash of 1929 only exacerbated Germany's mounting economic problems, which attracted the Communists, who decided this was a perfect opportunity to take advantage of the country's vulnerability and overthrow the Socialist government. It was a chaotic, uncertain, frightening era in German history, with its hardworking people pushing wheelbarrows full of *reichsmarks* (now-worthless German money) for miles just to buy a simple loaf of bread. The nation needed a savior.

So along came this articulate, ambitious, physically unimposing man named Adolf Hitler. Passionately opposed to the widely resented Versailles treaty. The guts to stand up to the Communists. Remedies for the foundering economy. Positive, optimistic, a fervent nationalist, promising unity and the restoration of order to a once-strong, once-proud society in urgent need of the help he was offering.

And sure enough, almost immediately after Hitler took charge, Germany's recovery was under way. There was no more rabble-rousing in the streets, no more criminality, no more long lines in front of stores and bakeries, no more rampant, crippling unemployment, and a wealth of glowing daily reports in the German press about all of it, thanks to Hitler's vast, carefully orchestrated propaganda machine.

At that time, in that context, it's not hard to imagine why Hitler seemed like the answer to Germany's prayers; why my father and millions of other good, decent Germans joined the Nazi Party; and why it's not a contradiction that never so much as a racist, anti-Semitic word was uttered in my father's household, nor was anti-Semitism even an issue.

When World War II ended an English Allied officer came to our house, arrested my father, and took him to prison to be "denazified," a common fate among members of the Nazi Party who were in positions of authority and, like my father, too old to be drafted into the military during the war. He was gone for a year, and I remember as if it were yesterday the sunny afternoon when my brothers and I were called indoors from a makeshift game of soccer to welcome home a father we adored and had missed so much.

I was six years old when I joyfully threw my arms around his neck that day, too young to understand where he'd been and why, or what had happened to make all those terrifying bombs stop exploding around us. Like a typical boy of six, I was too preoccupied with school, friends, and sports.

Throughout my life, sports have been my salvation, in more ways than I can ever express. Far beyond just being an outlet for an excess of energy and an innate competitive spirit, sports taught me discipline, and structure, and rules, and winning and losing with dignity, and the essential importance of never giving up. They gave me the perspective of knowing that no matter what the sport and how gifted I might be at it, there were always those I could beat and those who were better than I was, having nothing to do with what color or race they were. They instilled a perpetual, exhilarating sense of something to strive for, a steely internal awareness that even when I excelled, I might be able to do better if I worked and trained and tried harder than I was already doing.

Tanzschule, or dancing lessons, and gymnastics were mandatory for young German boys, so whether it was the waltz or the tango or backflips or routines on the pommel horse, I learned to appreciate the connection between a healthy, stimulated mind and a healthy, stimulated body. I developed strength and coordination and focus and confidence that I could never have found anywhere else.

My sports options were narrowed a bit by the four concussions I suffered in three years, starting when I was nine—one from the excitement of seeing my grandfather, which sent me racing down the stairs so fast that I forgot to compensate for the knee brace I was wearing; one from being pushed off the gymnastics horse; one from playing ice hockey on a frozen pond without a helmet, getting hit in the side of the head with a hockey stick, and then cracking the back of my head on the rock-hard ice when I fell; and one from a collision with a truck while I was dashing home on my bicycle. Each concussion required three weeks of bed rest, as a result of which I was held back in school, and I was strictly forbidden from playing contact sports ever again.

I swear I tried, but I didn't completely cooperate with that second command, fond as I was of our sweet, very capable country doctor. A Northern German Youth boxing champion transferred to my school and invited me to spar with him, and I admit it, I couldn't resist. I was no match for him, but he was impressed enough that he suggested I join his boxing club. I enjoyed it too much to turn down some training sessions here and there, doctor's orders aside, and I might have decided, with a young boy's logic, that it was worth the risk of permanent brain damage if a noncontact sport hadn't come along and captured my full attention.

I had the good fortune to fall in love with track and field, and to discover that I had the determination and the natural ability to excel at it. German schools taught physical education and various sports, but they didn't have teams. Instead, young gifted athletes were recruited by and trained at local athletic clubs, in exchange for membership fees. I quickly gravitated to discus, javelin, and shot put and trained almost obsessively. It paid off. Even now I look back on a day in 1958, when I won the German Youth Team Championship in discus, javelin, and shot put, and our small club, *Rendsburger* TSV, beat such powerhouses as Cologne, Munich, Berlin, and Hamburg, as one of the proudest moments of my life.

Years later, in America, as if they hadn't already enriched my life enough, sports would provide me with not only another national championship and a scholarship at the University of Montana but also a chance to atone in some small way for incomprehensible sins against humanity I knew nothing about until I left Germany.

ONE BITTERLY COLD NOVEMBER NIGHT WHEN I WAS TWELVE years old, my brothers and I were awakened out of a sound sleep by my mother crying out from the room next to ours.

My father had suffered a heart attack. The doctor arrived within a few short minutes, but it was too late. Impossibly, unspeakably, my father was dead.

It was the most defining, emotionally traumatic event of my life. From that instant on, nothing was ever the same. I was never the same.

As so often happens, especially when you're young and grief is sudden, my memories from those first days are nothing but the handful of brief, indelible images that managed to imprint themselves through the fog of shocked disbelief. Pulling back the sheet that covered my father's face before they took away his body, hoping, I guess, that I could find comfort, or relief, or hope, or some acceptable explanation with one more look at him. Sitting with my brothers at the very crowded funeral, unable to connect with where I was and why I was there. Standing in a receiving line with the rest of my family, woodenly shaking hands with an endless line of mourners whose condolences, sincere as I'm sure they were, sounded like nothing but distant noise.

It became a part of my life to take off on my bike alone and ride through the countryside to spend time at my father's grave, still trying to grasp that he was gone or feel some sign that he wasn't. "I'm going to make you proud," I'd whisper out loud, and it felt like a sacred promise because I was making it to him.

Within a few weeks we didn't just see the end of our life of privilege, we plunged into utter poverty. The Nazis had confiscated most of my father's trucks during the war. What trucks they didn't confiscate, the British did, when the war ended and they took over. Those devastating losses, compounded by his year of imprisonment, had left my father in debt, a fact that undoubtedly contributed to the heart attack that killed him.

Our big, beautiful house and grounds were sold, and we were moved to the second floor, reduced to being tenants in a small fragment of a home we'd once owned. My two older brothers were out on their own by then, so it was me, my younger brother, and my mother, with no central heating, no hot running water, no toilets that flushed, no shower, just the possessions we were able to salvage from what seemed like a whole other lifetime. Many of those possessions disappeared as well—a few times a month I would ride my bicycle to the pawnshop to ask if anything of ours had sold, in the hope of coming home with money to buy food. Christmas, which had always been a joyful holiday of family, feasts, and a thrilling array of presents, was suddenly hollow and sad. My brothers and I were still required to act out our long-cherished tradition of reciting poetry to the local Santa Claus and singing "O Tannenbaum" and "Stille Nacht, Heilige Nacht" before we could open our presents, but those presents were now reduced to, perhaps, a pair of shoes we were reminded would need to last until the next Christmas a year away. We still played soccer in the fields behind the house, but we had to improvise with a pig bladder because we could no longer afford a soccer ball.

It still amazes me that no amount of hardship, not even the loss of her husband and her shocking change of lifestyle, could cause my mother to sacrifice her pride and her dignity. Wealthy relatives would arrive for holidays and birthdays, climb the stairs to our cramped second-floor flat, and still be gracefully, generously served with the exquisite china and flatware Mother treasured from her past life. Everyone acted as if nothing had changed, nothing was different, and only once did any of those relatives offer to help, which I resented and don't understand to this day. She also kept up a favorite tradition of inviting a close friend or two, one of them a previous maid of ours, for four o'clock coffee and cake, until, without saying a word about it to us, she took a job at a factory, an unheard-of disgrace for the former first lady of our village.

My older brothers told me many, many years later that one of those close friends and that same maid who enjoyed my mother's determined hospitality had had affairs with our father. Whether or not Mother knew about them at the time I have no idea. I'm glad I didn't. I wouldn't have loved him one bit less, but I might have been disappointed in him, and heroes are so hard for young boys to come by.

It was an overwhelming number of changes for a twelve-year-old to process, especially one who was still mourning the loss of the most important person in his life, with no clue how to make sense of it.

Until track and field came along to rescue me, life was now

too hard for school to be enjoyable. I woke up every morning at five, in time to ride my bicycle, often through bone-chilling winds, to the train station for the forty-five-minute train ride to school. Then, after a long day at school, it was back on the train, back on my bicycle, and home to our small, cold flat, where there may or may not be food for dinner and I may or may not find enough energy for a bit of homework before falling into bed to rest up for more of the same the next morning. On weekends, I contributed to the household income as best I could by doing manual labor on nearby farms, which toughened me and made me stronger as much as it exhausted me. As an added bonus, farmwork gave me access to barbed-wire fences dotted with wool from sheep rubbing against them. I'd gather the bits of wool and take them home for my mother to weave into fabric, from which she made the world's most uncomfortable underwear. The wardrobe department of *The Young and the Restless* will back me up on this—sixty years later I still can't and won't tolerate scratchy clothing against my skin.

I wasn't raptly interested in every subject school had to offer, but I was an avid reader and especially good at English. From an early age, when school ceremonies included a poem or a literary passage, I was invariably chosen to perform the reading, with no idea that someday I'd find myself performing the written word for a living. In fact, I can honestly say that an acting career never once entered my mind until many years and thousands of miles later. I was content to accompany my mother to the small movie theater at a local inn and be enthralled by such actors as Germany's Curt Jürgens, France's Jean Gabin, and a couple of Americans who made especially powerful impressions on me: Clark Gable in *Gone with the Wind* (which my mother saw thirteen times) and Marlon Brando in *Julius Caesar.* If anyone had told me I would work with Brando someday on a film called *Moratori,* I would have thought they were insane. I was much too busy back then just making it from one day to the next and dealing with the rage that started filling the void my father left behind.

I remember the exact moment when I felt rage for the first time.

Rage was never a part of the almost daily fights I had with my brothers. We were four healthy, rowdy, strong-willed, competitive boys, each of whom wanted his way in any disagreement and didn't find it either satisfying or efficient to calmly talk things through. There was always a tacit understanding among us that we loved each other and would have defended each other to the death against any outsider who dared to take one of us on, so as hard as we sometimes fought, it never got out of hand.

It wasn't even part of the constant fights I had with a boy known as Dickie (real name Paul Johannsen) who lived next door. We didn't like each other, and we couldn't seem to be within fifty feet of each other without a fight breaking out. But those fights weren't about doing serious damage to each other, they were simply ongoing exercises in the spirit of *quien es mas macho* between neighbors.

Rage crystallized in me one night after my father was gone, when I happened to overhear one of his former drivers making insulting comments about him. I'd never felt such blind, white-hot anger before, or been so completely overwhelmed with contempt for another human being. I would have given anything to see my father come down and beat that man to a bloody pulp. As it was, I was too young and too small to take him on myself, so I didn't say a word or lay a hand on him, but a fire was lit in me that night that I still haven't completely extinguished.

I began to get in fights at school, usually with arrogant older bullies—never with any boy who was smaller or weaker than I was. The most memorable happened one day after gymnastics class, when a self-proclaimed tough guy challenged me. My adrenaline and hormones were racing by the time I knocked him out, so that when the gymnastics coach angrily rushed in to restrain me, I instinctively turned on him, raised my fists, and yelled, "You want some too?" We didn't come to blows, but I was fully prepared to take him on.

While I still don't completely understand it, I think there was, and still is, something deeply offensive to me about anyone who seems to feel arrogantly entitled to take up more than their fair share of space, who carries around a smug sense of superiority without the credentials to back it up. I was also fourteen at the time, an age when we're all trying to find our place in this world, and continuing to struggle with the loss of a father who'd always given me the privilege of unconditional respect, and I wasn't about to give up being respected without as many fights as it took.

My mother, by the way, put the school principal in his place that day when he threatened to expel me. Like a lioness defending her cub, she marched into his office and asked him, "How do you think that I, as a widow, can handle four boys when you can't even handle one?"

Once again, sports saved me—it was around that time that I joined the track-and-field team. Without that outlet for my rage, given my surging hormones and my general fearlessness, I shudder to think where I might have ended up.

Not all the battles I was fighting in those days were physical ones. I was also actively looking for a spiritual belief system that made sense to me.

I was raised Protestant. I knew all the principles of Christianity by heart. It was when I stopped memorizing them and started questioning them that I ran into trouble.

I wasn't shy about asking those questions—I genuinely wanted to learn and understand and be enlightened on the subject of God in ways I could apply to my life. I had inquisitive talks with the church elders. I took long walks with a devout older woman who lived nearby and had enough faith to fill a hundred churches. I read tirelessly about a variety of religious theories, from the manuscripts of German philosopher Friedrich Nietzsche to the works of theologian, philosopher, and medical missionary Dr. Albert Schweitzer, who devoted much of his life to working in the leper colonies of Africa and whom I admired very much.

The more questions I asked, the more questions I thought of, but they could probably be distilled down to just two basic ones: How could a benevolent Father allow something as horrific as war? And if God is omnipotent, as you say He is, that means He chose to take away my father and leave my mother with such a hard life. Why would He do such a thing to a family who so faithfully loved and honored Him?

Sincere and poetic as the answers usually were, I found them wanting.

I'm still asking, still reading, still wondering, still searching.

So far I can say with absolute certainty that I believe in two basic principles of the Christian faith I was taught from childhood: the notion of forgiveness, and our responsibility as citizens of this earth to serve those less fortunate than we are.

Beyond that, I tend to embrace a precept of Saint Augustine: "I doubt, therefore I am."

Thankfully, while I took my internal journeys seriously, I didn't let them interfere with the two most compelling passions of my high school years, passions that gave me some of my happiest times in Germany: sports and girls. And since we athletes seemed to have our pick of the local girls, I never had to choose one passion over the other. In fact, they seemed to complement each other perfectly.

I loved track-and-field practice and the thrilling adrenaline rush that came from improving at it and continuing to surpass what I thought was my own personal best. I still recall not just the day but the specific moment when I threw a javelin over fifty meters for the first time. Of course, as far as our team was concerned, track and field was the best sport in school, and we were the *crème de la crème* of athletes—we could run faster, jump higher, and throw farther than all the others. That there was usually a crowd of girls watching us practice gave us even more incentive to try harder and show off, knowing we'd be rewarded with a lot of female attention later, and I was only too happy to take full advantage of it.

One day when I was fifteen a new girl appeared in the crowd at one of our track meets. She went to another school and was there with friends from her school. She asked about me, I found out later, and was told that while I was a bit of a Don Juan, I had a few things going for me, and she ended up inviting me and my teammates to a dinner party at the home of a wealthy elderly woman.

It was a beautiful house, and we boys and our dates wore our best evening wear. Shortly after we arrived, the new girl showed up in a Mercedes with an "older man" in his early twenties.

You know those sweet, rare moments when you make eye contact with someone and you're both aware without saying a word that something is happening between you? She sat diagonally across the table from me, and we shared that moment. When we'd finished our meal I asked her to dance. We never sat down again, letting Elvis Presley and Louis Armstrong and Count Basie propel us through a magical, almost wordless evening during which, for the first time, I fell in love.

Her name was Rosely. It turned out that our wealthy hostess that night was her grandmother, and her father was one of the wealthiest men in Germany. She was elegant and unpretentious and utterly enchanting. She'd pick me up on Sundays in her Mercedes, always coming upstairs to say hello to Mother, never seeming to notice or care about the sharp contrast between her exquisite home and our cramped, threadbare flat. We'd take long walks in the countryside and stop for picnics and urgent, adolescent kisses, and I treasured every minute I spent with her, just as I treasured her letters throughout my first lonely years in America.

When I was seventeen my mother, younger brother, and I went to Hamburg to visit my mother's sister. Her three daughters, my cousins, were brilliantly accomplished women, and the middle one, an oncologist, was visiting from Texas. By the time the afternoon ended, she'd offered to sponsor me and give me a place to stay if I'd like to go to the United States after I graduated from high school.

Like most German boys my age, I'd read my share of Karl May's adventure novels about the American West, so Texas sounded like paradise on earth to me. I had no idea what I wanted to do there—maybe become a cowboy and make friends with a lot of Indians, who were always heroes in Karl May's books. My highest marks in school were in English, and Germany was still struggling to its feet, while the United States was prospering. I was seventeen years old, an age when playing it safe was a foreign concept. I was curious. I was wide open to new experiences and unexplored paths, wherever they led. And I had a year to finish high school and get ready for the most extraordinary journey of my young life.

That year flew past while I studied, practiced my English, worked hard on farms and at the local sawmill to earn my passage, and dutifully filled out the necessary paperwork at the American consulate in Hamburg. Before I knew it, I'd graduated and packed my bags and was holding back tears as best I could as I said a very emotional good-bye to my mother, my brothers, my girlfriend, my country, and everything I knew of this world.

A band played "Junge, Komm Bald Wieder," which roughly translates to "Boy, Come Back Soon," while I walked up the gangway and boarded the SS *Hanseatic.* It was May of 1959. I was eighteen years old, with fifty hard-earned dollars in my pocket, already homesick but anxiously looking forward to whatever lay ahead as the *Hanseatic* transported me across the Atlantic to America and the rest of my life.

2

COMING TO AMERICA

I remember the smell of the ocean, mixed with the odor of too many people and the ship's fuel, as Germany slowly disappeared in the wake of the SS *Hanseatic.*

I remember the inevitable discovery that one mile of the Atlantic looks very much like the mile before it, eliminating the temptation to pass the time sightseeing.

And I remember almost immediately noticing her.

She was an older woman of twenty-five. She was beautiful, she seemed to be traveling alone, and she excited me.

I needed to level the maturity and sophistication playing fields between us if I was to stand a chance with her. Fortunately, I'd seen my share of Humphrey Bogart movies, so I knew exactly what to do—I bought my first pack of cigarettes and made sure she saw me smoking.

It worked.

She was one very experienced, very enthusiastic twenty-five-year-old, and I was one very lucky eighteen-year-old, until I was sidelined three days into the trip by a decidedly unsophisticated bout of seasickness, giving new meaning to the farewell cliché "It's not you, it's me."

Finally, at six one morning, we passengers were all summoned to the deck to witness our breathtaking approach to the Statue of Liberty, with the New York skyline as its backdrop. It was overwhelming for a young man from a small German village, one of those sights that somehow make you feel humble and invincible at the same time.

The statue's eloquent Emma Lazarus inscription ran through my mind over and over again as the *Hanseatic* entered the harbor:

Give me your tired, your poor,
Your huddled masses yearning to breathe free,
The wretched refuse of your teeming shore.
Send these, the homeless, tempest-tossed to me,
I lift my lamp beside the golden door!

What a compassionate welcome, I thought. What a magnificent country this must be.

My cousin Wiebke, a successful psychiatrist, was waiting for me at the Thirty-Fourth Street docks that morning. She greeted me with a warm, familiar embrace that felt like home, exactly when I needed it, and then took me on a tour of the tall, noisy city. The frenetic hustle and bustle of white and black and brown-skinned people were as curious to me as any of the tourist attractions we visited.

We had lunch in an eatery at the top of the Empire State Building. I studied the menu and paid special attention to the prices so I could carefully allocate the fifty dollars that was all I had to my name. A cheeseburger and a chocolate milk shake seemed affordable, but I had another concern.

As a psychiatrist, Wiebke obviously had a medical degree, so I assumed she'd studied nutrition. "Are these good for you?" I asked her.

She answered with a passing yes.

I adhered to a strict diet of cheeseburgers and milk shakes for weeks.

I was fortunate enough to have another cousin, Maren, who taught at the University of Texas Medical School in Galveston and had a job waiting for me in Texas, so next thing I knew I was embarking on a three-day trip from New York City to Galveston on a Greyhound bus.

It was late May, getting warmer and steamier by the day as we headed into the deep South. The Greyhound only stopped in the poorest sections of the towns along the way, and I was mystified by the bus depot drinking fountains—some were marked WHITES and some were marked COLOREDS. What the hell could that be about? Did those drinking fountains dispense different water? And if so, why? It couldn't be something as obscene as segregation, not in a country that threw its arms open to "your tired, your poor, your huddled masses yearning to breathe free." But I was new to America, still a guest in someone else's home, so I politely never asked.

On one leg of the journey I sat next to a Southern woman who was intrigued by her young German seatmate. She was especially curious to know what I thought of Adolf Hitler. I had no idea what would prompt her to ask. I knew Germany had lost World War II, almost fifteen years ago, when I was four years old. Of what possible interest could Hitler be to her or anyone else a decade and a half later?

Texas was vast and sweltering, with occasional herds of grazing cattle but an odd lack of cowboys as the Greyhound lumbered its way to Galveston. My doctor cousin Maren and her husband Jan Bakker had generously invited me to stay with them, and the job she'd secured for me started the very next morning. A colleague of hers, a pathologist, was studying arthritis. My assignment, for eight hours a day, was to cut open the knee joints of the corpses in the hospital's cadaver hall for him to examine.

There was no air-conditioning. There were no fans. It was just me, scalpel in hand, sweat pouring off of me, in a large room full of dead people, more than willing to earn my keep but not believing for a moment that I'd found my life's calling.

I'd devised a whole new plan for my future by the time we relocated to Dallas a few weeks later—I decided to become a United States Marine. From what I'd heard, Marines were well paid, with a rock-solid code of honor and a rigorous emphasis on physical fitness. What could possibly go wrong? I went straight to the nearest recruiting office, ready and eager to be a Marine when I walked out a few hours later.

Unfortunately, there was the little matter of a written test I hadn't seen coming. I failed it miserably. I'd studied English in school, and I did very well at it. What I hadn't begun to learn after only seven weeks in America was how to convert the metric system I'd grown up with to the United States' system of weights and measurements. Miles vs. kilometers? Who knows? Pounds vs. kilograms, or knots vs. miles per hour? Not a clue. Fahrenheit vs. Celsius? Beats me.

The recruiter was very encouraging—he understood the problem, and he could see that in general I was smart and very motivated. He suggested that I work on those areas of the test I'd struggled with and try again in six months, when he was sure I'd pass with flying colors and be a credit to the Marine Corps.

I might have done exactly that if, less than six months later, I hadn't moved on to a whole new adventure more than a thousand miles away.

It was apparent to my cousin that I was restless and eager to get some traction in my life, so she sent a telegram on my behalf to a friend of hers. He was an eighty-year-old German expatriate who'd come to America in 1900. He owned a ranch in Montana, and yes, he replied, he could always use another ranch hand, starting as soon as I could get there.

A ranch meant wide-open spaces and a lot of the physical labor I grew up on and was yearning for. In a perfect world, it might even mean a chance to become a cowboy. As far as I was concerned, at that moment, on that day, it really was a perfect world. I virtually raced to the nearest bus station and headed north.

The countryside between Texas and Montana was breathtaking, some of the most magnificent I'd ever seen, which is why it didn't just offend me, it outraged me that it was littered all along the way with huge, garish billboards. I was horrified that any corporation, no matter how greedy, would feel entitled to intrude on such sacredly pristine beauty.

Thankfully, I wasn't alone in my disgust. A few years later, in 1965, Lady Bird Johnson, wife of President Lyndon Johnson, spearheaded America's Highway Beautification Act to control outdoor advertising, roadside junkyards, and interstate highway landscaping. We all owe her an enormous debt of gratitude.

My cousin's rancher friend met me at the Missoula, Montana, bus station in his brand-new Chevy and took me home to introduce me to his family and show me my room. Bright and early the next morning, I met the other ranch hands and we were given our work orders for the day. And then, without fanfare, my longtime dream came true—we were each assigned a horse. All those boyhood years of watching westerns and voraciously reading novels about the Old West, all those youthful fantasies of living the rugged, fearless life of an American cowboy, came to fruition as I mounted that horse and took the reins.

I learned something interesting about all those cowboy movies and novels on my first day of work on the ranch—they conveniently failed to mention the agony of going from zero hours a day on horseback to eight hours a day on horseback. I wasn't sure I'd ever walk normally again.

But somehow the searing pain in my lower body didn't stop me from joining the other ranch hands in racing our horses back to the barn at a full gallop as the sun set, for which we were scolded by our boss at the top of his lungs on those occasions when he caught us at it.

For the most part, though, I was in my element, baling hay, chopping wood, hauling feed, repairing fences and outbuildings, driving cattle down from the mountains, feeling one hundred percent alive and loving everything about that ranch except the constant, pervasive smell of skunks I never did learn to appreciate.

One of the more memorable nights of my cowboy era began at a party held by a neighboring rancher. He happened to have a very attractive daughter, and after spending the evening flirting, we quietly agreed to meet at a secluded spot between the two ranches at eleven.

It was a beautiful night. We each arrived on horseback, in

the silence of a vast countryside, under a half-moon and a sky full of stars that reached all the way to the horizon.

We were just beginning to enjoy ourselves and each other when we heard our horses nervously whinnying and looked up to discover that we were being approached by a large, hungry-looking brown bear.

I'm fearless, but I'm not a fool. We were long gone before I even began to wonder how one goes about chasing away a bear.

I was told that Montana State University, now the University of Montana, offered track-and-field scholarships. With my track-and-field skills and my contribution to the German Youth Team Championship in discus, javelin, and shot put, I decided to give it a try. I had a meeting with the coach and tried out for the team, and a few days later an acceptance letter arrived from the university. I felt as if I'd just won the lottery. As grateful as I was for my time on the ranch, I was more than ready to trade it in for the life of an athlete and scholar.

In the beginning I loved everything about it. I've always been very intellectually curious, and it felt wonderful to have my mind stimulated again by the courses required for my chosen majors of political science and economics. In fact, one of my humanities professors was the brilliant, eloquent Leslie Fiedler, who went on to become a prolific author, critic, and provocateur.

I joined ROTC, the Reserve Officers Training Corps, predawn drill practice and all, with the goal in mind that after college I'd join the armed forces at an elevated status.

Between my track-and-field teammates and the campus fraternity that was courting me, I made friends with fellow students from all over the world. We talked endlessly about sports and classes and, of course, women, from our unanimous approval of tight sweaters to our confusion over the fact that American girls seemed to smile at us a great deal without meaning a damned thing by it.

I also had a girlfriend, whom I met at a fraternity party when we serenaded her sorority house. Her name was Dorothy McBride. She was a smart, attractive fellow student, and it's come as no surprise that she's now a notable academic.

It all started so perfectly, until harsh reality brought it crashing down around me.

My partial track-and-field scholarship covered tuition, nothing more. All other expenses were my responsibility, and I had no money. I needed a place to live, and I was an invited guest in a campus fraternity house on University Avenue for a month, presumably in the hope that I'd join the fraternity. But there was no way I could afford it, nor, I'd decided after that month, was it of any interest to me. I managed to find affordable housing in the home of a German graduate student in forestry and his American wife, who taught German literature. That sweet couple, the Nonnenmachers, rented me a space in their basement next to the water heater, and I was damned glad to have it.

I also needed a job, and I was quickly hired by a nearby lumber mill, on the six P.M. to two A.M. shift. Eighteen-wheeler trucks would bring huge tree trunks to the mill to be sawed into boards by "green chains." I was part of two teams of ten men each who stood on either side of the green chains to pull the boards through and stack them, in a huge building that consisted of a roof supported by poles but no walls and no protection from the oncoming bitter cold.

And so, beginning in September of 1959, my schedule became so brutal it almost broke me.

I'd work until two A.M., sink into bed in my basement room at around three, and catch what sleep I could until it was time to leave for eight A.M. classes, except for those days when I fulfilled my early-morning ROTC drill-team obligations. Classes and lectures continued until one P.M., when track-and-field practice started. After practice, I'd have something to eat and do my best to study for an hour or two before heading back to the lumber mill for my six P.M. shift.

I was a young, healthy, motivated man, but that relentless routine quickly took a toll on every aspect of my life. With so little time for homework, I was barely passing my courses. I became too underfed and exhausted to excel at track and field. A friend persuaded me to audition for a university production of Anton Chekhov's *The Cherry Orchard*, which intrigued me—the idea of being an actor had never occurred to me, but I'd always excelled at reading poetry and classical literature aloud in school throughout my childhood, and I needed to feel good at something again. I got the part and had to turn it down. I barely had time to eat, sleep, or study. Finding time for rehearsals and performances was laughably impossible.

One of my professors invited a few of us foreign students to speak to a class about our respective homelands. During the question-and-answer part of the hour, I was asked, "How could a country that produced the likes of Beethoven, and Einstein, and Bertolt Brecht, and Albert Schweitzer produce Adolf Hitler?" I couldn't imagine how to respond to that. I still can't. But at the time it felt like a sucker punch.

Life seemed bleak, as if I were on a hamster wheel, running as hard as I could, going nowhere, with no purpose and no end in sight. I'd managed to save two hundred dollars from my lumber-mill pay and spent every dime on a late-night call to Rosely in Germany, the one person who could calm me and remind me that I wasn't as lost as I felt.

I was in that frame of mind, at the end of my first year at Montana State, when, through mutual friends, I met a fellow student named Bob McKinnon. He was a big, burly outdoorsman, a character Ernest Hemingway would have been proud to create. He was a collegiate swimmer and an experienced river rafter who had a fascination with the Lewis and Clark Expedition. He'd rafted from North Fork, Idaho, to Oakland, California, and from Benton, Montana, to Savannah, Georgia, and I liked and admired him.

One day he approached me with a very unexpected proposal: he was preparing for a trip to traverse Idaho's Salmon

River, described by Lewis and Clark as "foaming and roaring through rocks in every direction, so as to render the passage of anything impossible." Pioneers who'd managed to make their way upriver had found the currents too strong to navigate their way back to the sites where their journeys began, so that an eighty-five-mile stretch of the Salmon became known as "The River of No Return."

McKinnon's intention was to become the first man ever to successfully complete a round trip on the River of No Return, and he wanted me to join him.

"I've asked a few other people," he said, "but they turned me down."

I was too intrigued to ask why. Instead, I simply asked, "What's the upshot?"

"The trip's being sponsored by Crestliner Boats, Johnson Motors, and Alcoa Aluminum, and we're making a documentary of it called *The Riverbusters*. Once the film's finished, we'll go to Los Angeles and find a distributor."

I had no clue what I'd be getting into if I said yes, but I knew very well what I'd be getting out of—a life that was dragging me down and seemed to be going nowhere.

With the simple words "Let's do it," and a handshake, I was off on a whole new adventure that just kept on going and impossibly, in the end, led to my acting career.

We left Missoula towing the fifteen-foot Crestliner boat on the back of Bob McKinnon's old Chevrolet. Four and a half hours later we arrived in Lewiston, Idaho, and its twin city,

Clarkston, Washington, directly across the Snake River, downstream from the Salmon, where the chamber of commerce had arranged a press conference for us. The attention and the excitement were overwhelming and more than a little unnerving—the Salmon wasn't called the River of No Return for nothing, after all, and this many people gathering to watch two guys try to conquer it meant it really might be impossible, if not utterly insane. McKinnon had plenty of expertise in traversing rivers all over the country and was in great physical shape. He'd coached me exhaustively, and I was athletically skilled enough to tackle pretty much anything. But so many had tried and failed on this same journey. Who exactly did we think we were?

The water was very still at our starting point, surrounded by pristine wilderness and towering rock walls of a canyon more than five thousand feet deep. It was easy to understand why the Nez Percé Indians who'd inhabited this land for centuries considered it sacred. It did stir my soul.

We began to hear a loud roar ahead of us that became cacophonous when we rounded a bend and found ourselves facing the first rapid . . . massive, roiling, and palpably powerful, a true "holy shit!" moment.

McKinnon circled around in front of it, stalking it like a hunter, deciding where to attack. Finally he maneuvered us into position, yelled, "Hold on!" and gunned the motor. We flew forward and hit the rapid full force. It was like hitting a wall—we went nowhere.

He backed up, and we unloaded all the gas tanks. I gathered

them and climbed across the rocks to the other side of the rapid as McKinnon hit it again in the much lighter Crestliner. He threaded his way through the angry white water inch by inch until he finally blasted through it with a roar as loud as the river.

We were jubilant. We were invincible. We couldn't wait for the next rapid.

Native Americans believe that all of nature is as alive as we are, a living, breathing creation to be revered and nurtured. I came to agree. The Salmon became almost human to me—not an enemy, but a fierce, worthy competitor, arrogantly protecting itself from being conquered, and proud of its perfect record. There could be only one winner in this fight, us or the river, and I'd be damned if it was going to be that river.

It was a long, grueling, exhilarating trip.

McKinnon and I began taking turns jumping into the river to swim the rapids while the other took the boat through them.

I was sure I was going to drown when the boat became stuck on the rocks and tipped over with me trapped underneath it. McKinnon swam ashore and jumped down on the boat to dislodge it, and I was catapulted into the air by the force of the white water when he succeeded.

Twice our propeller shaft broke on rocks hidden beneath the river's surface. On one of those occasions we spent a few days on the banks of the Salmon near White Bird, waiting for parts to arrive from Granville. Several of the local women came to check us out, immediately followed by several of the local men, who weren't one bit happy about the attention we were getting from "their" women and tried unsuccessfully to bring us down a notch or two.

Other than that, our only breaks were a few occasional hours in our sleeping bags here and there, when we'd sometimes be too exhausted to sleep. The press was tracking our journey, as was our filmmaker, a professional photographer from Missoula, who only managed to capture what was probably the calmest mile of the trip. *Life* magazine had planned to do a story on us, but by the time we made our turn at Riggins, Idaho, and fought our way back to Lewiston-Clarkston after three hard, thrilling, unforgettable weeks, we were a week later than expected and a week too late for *Life*'s deadline.

It didn't matter. We'd done it. We'd won. Battered, bruised, and bone-tired, we'd become the first men to traverse the River of No Return from its source to its mouth and back again, and the overwhelming sense of accomplishment was and still is indescribable.

The only casualty from that once-in-a-lifetime adventure was a pendant and chain Rosely had given me. I'd never taken it off from the day she gave it to me, and it was apparently swallowed up by that fierce water. I hated losing it but kind of liked knowing that something important to me and so close to my heart would always remain at the site of one of my most treasured memories.

After a large, boisterous celebration thrown for us by the

Lewiston-Clarkston Chamber of Commerce, McKinnon and I hitched our Crestliner to the back of his Chevy and headed back to a huge "hometown" heroes' welcome in Missoula.

A few months later the documentary of our trip was completed to our satisfaction. We called it *The Riverbusters*, and we were enormously proud of it and excited about it when, as planned, we boarded a Greyhound and set off to find a distributor in Los Angeles, which sounded like as good a place as any to set up camp temporarily while I tried to figure out what on earth to do next.

3

FROM PARKING CARS TO BROADWAY

It was late summer of 1960, warm and smoggy, when we arrived in Los Angeles by way of Santa Barbara on the Pacific coast. The huge international advertising firm J. Walter Thompson sent a man named Bill Prentiss to meet our bus in downtown L.A. and deliver us to their offices.

We were greeted with flattering enthusiasm and an unexpected offer. It seems Johnson Motors and Alcoa Aluminum were so impressed with our success on the Salmon River that they wanted to provide us with a larger boat and sponsor us to tackle the Amazon, one of the two longest rivers in the world.

Tempted as I'm sure he was, McKinnon had to say no—his girlfriend Suzy was pregnant, and he wasn't about to leave her for a lengthy, potentially dangerous trip to South America. If he wasn't going, I certainly wasn't going, so we had to say thanks, but no thanks. We were paid for our River of No Return adventure, McKinnon headed off in search of a distributor for *The Riverbusters,* and my five-hundred-dollar check and I were on our own in a strange new city with no reason to return to Montana, particularly with winter just a few short months away.

I checked in to a little motel at Burton Way and San Vicente, on the outskirts of Beverly Hills and across from what's known in L.A. as Restaurant Row. I quickly got a job as a valet, at $1.25 an hour. (All tips went to the owner of the parking concession.) It had its benefits—I've had a passion for cars, and speed, since I was ten years old, and the other valets and I had a great time racing Ferraris, Rolls-Royces, Maseratis, and Lamborghinis down the ramp to the parking structure.

I supplemented that income for a while as a mover for Bekins Moving and Storage, worth mentioning only because of an epiphanous moment when I learned the most effective English swearword I'd ever heard.

An older coworker and I were struggling up a narrow interior stairway carrying a large refrigerator. For some reason the refrigerator's owner, an unpleasant woman with an equally unpleasant voice, felt compelled to stand at the top of the stairs and shriek at us not to crash the refrigerator into the wall, as if we wouldn't have tried to avoid that without her supervision.

Finally, on about her fifth or sixth repetition about the wall, my coworker barked back, "Lady, would you shut the fuck up?"

That word could be used as a noun? I had no idea! It was efficient, it was emphatic, and I loved everything about it. I've made good use of it ever since.

I found a small apartment on Clark Street just below Sunset Boulevard. My landlords were a sweet elderly couple from Tennessee who'd invite me into their home to watch *Lawrence Welk* with them.

There was a drugstore nearby called Gil Turner's. It's still there, and I occasionally drive past it and remember my first Christmas Eve in Los Angeles. It was eighty degrees, a welcome change from the brutality of winter in Montana but a million miles from my beloved Germany. I celebrated the holiday with a small gift from my mother, letters from Rosely that meant the world to me, and a slow, agonizing walk to Gil Turner's with a nasty case of the flu to buy orange juice and Mounds candy bars.

A few weeks later I landed a valet job at Scandia, one of the most popular A-list restaurants in Hollywood at the time. Everyone from the Rat Pack to Marilyn Monroe to Warren Beatty and Natalie Wood hung out there, as did Paul and Walter Kohner, whose talent agency was the biggest in town for foreign actors. The Kohner brothers represented the likes of Marlene Dietrich, Maurice Chevalier, Greta Garbo, Max von Sydow, and Ingmar Bergman; and whenever they showed up at Scandia, my fellow valets would push me to introduce myself. An endless number of postwar television and film projects were being shot in the early 1960s, and authentic German actors were in huge demand. I wasn't an actor, or even an aspiring one, but I wasn't planning to be a valet for the rest of my life either, so why not have the highly respected Kohner brothers submit me for some roles and see what happened?

I had to admit, it sounded like it might be worth a try. I certainly had nothing to lose.

I lied to the Kohner brothers when I met them and told them that yes, of course I'd acted in Germany before I came to America. They wisely had me audition for them, and, grateful yet again for having excelled at reading classical literature aloud in school, I read some poetry or something, just well enough that they signed me on as a client.

My first audition was for a B movie called *Operation Eichmann,* starring the late Werner Klemperer, about the capture of Nazi war criminal Adolf Eichmann in Argentina. I met the producers, I did a cold reading for them, and I got the part—a very small part, but my first acting job nonetheless.

Never has the word "novice" been more of an understatement.

A script arrived. I didn't know what I was supposed to do with it, so I set it aside without so much as a glance.

Then pages of various colors began to arrive—blue one day, yellow another, pink another, green another. I couldn't begin to guess what those were about and simply threw them away. (It took me another job or two to learn that script revisions are color-coded, and the new colored pages are meant to replace the color before them.)

My day of filming arrived. I had no idea where the Hal Roach Studio at MGM was, and I was too broke to take a cab.

And so, for my Hollywood acting debut, I arrived on a city bus, an hour and a half late.

I'd never been on a film set before. I was gaping around at the confounding foreignness of it when someone rushed up and led me to a nearby trailer with an urgent "We've got to get you into hair and makeup."

Of course, I acted as if I couldn't have been more accustomed to all this, but hair and *what*? Were they kidding?

Once that strange ordeal was over with, another someone hurried me onto the set. The director, R. G. Springsteen, quickly and politely introduced himself and then instructed me that "when Werner crosses from over here, you meet him there and say your lines."

I nodded sagely, not having understood a word he said. I'd turned ice-cold inside, thinking, "I am so fucked."

I fought the urge to run away as fast as I could and instead stood there, still as a statue. Minutes later someone yelled, "Action!"

Moments after that someone yelled, "Cut!"

I wondered how I could have possibly done something wrong so soon, without even taking a breath. To my profound relief, the problem was a camera malfunction. Everyone around me seemed to relax and go about their business. I remained frozen in place, bracing myself for the inevitable moment when I'd be exposed, on camera and in front of all these people, as a complete impostor.

Then a woman approached me, gently touched my arm, and asked, "Do you know what you're supposed to say?"

There was no annoyed edge to her voice, nothing accusatory, nothing but compassion. All my bravado vanished. "No," I confessed, "I don't."

For the next twenty minutes, while the camera problem was being solved, this woman worked with me, patiently walking me through my lines and blocking until I had it down.

They started filming again, and Werner Klemperer and I got through the scene in one take. By all accounts I did a good job, and my agents were very impressed.

From that day forward, I've believed, and always will, that I owe my career to that woman. Her name was Bobbie Sierks, and she was the script supervisor on *Operation Eichmann*. If she hadn't been so kind and so helpful to me, my first job would have been my last—my agents would have heard I was unreliable and had arrived unprepared, and they would never have sent me on another audition.

Bobbie Sierks died in 1978. I deeply regret that I never took the time to track her down and tell her how indebted I am to her.

Operation Eichmann was quickly followed by two episodes of *The Gallant Men*, an ABC series about a company of American soldiers in Italy during World War II. I played the role of a radio operator—not very challenging, but I was grateful for the experience and the paycheck, and very impressed to meet Roland La Starza. As far as I was concerned, the fact that he was one of the series regulars was nothing compared to the fact that he was a retired boxer who'd once fought Rocky Marciano for a world heavyweight championship. To this day, given a choice between hanging out with a roomful of actors or a roomful of athletes, I'll choose the athletes every time.

The novelty of having a little extra money in my pocket from acting jobs felt like an unbelievable luxury. Not since I was twelve years old, when my father's death sent us into poverty, had I known that modicum of freedom from having to think about every dollar I spent and worry that it might compromise my upcoming rent payment. I wasn't earning enough to change my lifestyle or to give up my day job, but it was enough to allow a bit of an exhale and even a bit of optimism.

I developed enough confidence, and/or guts, to walk into auditions and ask to read for a bigger part than the one the producers and casting directors had in mind for me. It got me cast in six episodes of the popular World War II series *Combat*, and more often than not, it kept on working until I had enough of a track record to be offered bigger parts in the first place.

Not that my track record didn't have a bump or two along the way. It's amazing that my shiny new reputation didn't take a serious hit after my utterly humiliating guest appearance on an episode of a short-lived series called *Blue Light*.

Blue Light was set in—where else?—World War II Germany. It starred Robert Goulet as a double agent posing as an American traitor. I barely glanced at the script when it arrived, assuming it wouldn't take me long to learn a few lines of the usual Nazi drivel, so I arrived on the set very poorly prepared.

Only then did I discover that I was playing a spy. And not just any spy, mind you, but a spy who, for reasons I can't begin to recall, had page after page of dialogue about two subjects I knew and cared nothing about: baseball and mathematics. It was hopeless. Even when I'd manage to deliver a few lines without stammering or going completely blank, I didn't have the faintest idea what I was talking about. It was torture, for me and, I'm sure, for everyone else involved. It took me twenty takes to get through it. *Twenty takes.* Not before or since can I remember being so professionally embarrassed.

And then there was one of my more memorable meetings, for a film called *What Did You Do in the War, Daddy?*

By that time I had enough auditioning experience under my belt to know at least a few of the ropes, and I'd made what I thought was a very reasonable request of my agent: no cattle calls. In case you're not familiar with the term, a cattle call happens when a producer or casting director has absolutely no vision whatsoever for the role in question and, as a result, tells every agent in town to send in every client and their grandmother for the initial meeting. Cattle calls are kind of the "throw enough shit against the wall" approach to casting, and they demean every actor who has the misfortune to show up and sit in the reception area waiting hours for their two minutes' worth of bored, perfunctory attention.

I'd been assured that my meeting for *What Did You Do in the War, Daddy?* wasn't a cattle call, so we were already off to a bad start when I arrived to discover a crowded room packed with every German actor in the greater Los Angeles area.

I resisted the temptation to walk right back out. According

to my agent, this film was being directed by the enormously successful Blake Edwards, whose *Pink Panther* movies with Peter Sellers were the talk of the town. Impressing Blake Edwards, my agent assured me, could be a very good career move.

So instead of leaving, I signed in and said to the receptionist, "Tell them they've got five minutes."

Less than five minutes later I was shown into a private office. Three producers were sitting there, along with an acquaintance of mine, a Bavarian actor named Horst Ebersberg. And behind the large desk in this dimly lit room sat a man in a short-sleeved shirt, wearing sunglasses and holding a riding crop, looking like a cartoon.

I greeted Horst and asked, in German, what he was doing there.

"I'm here to make sure the German we cast can really speak German," he explained.

I was incredulous. We northern Germans have a longstanding tradition of laughing at the Bavarian dialect, and they hired a Bavarian to judge the authenticity of anyone's ability to speak German? Were they kidding?

But I had a far more pressing question for Horst—again in German, I asked, "Who is this idiot behind the desk?"

"That's our director."

I was done. "Tell that arrogant asshole I want nothing to do with this," I said, and I walked out.

Horst told me later that the instant I left, Blake Edwards turned to the producers and said, "I want him."

Thank you, but no, thank you. That movie and I went on without each other, and it was a decision I've never regretted.

We foreign actors tended to gravitate toward each other, and I got a call one day from an Austrian actor named Norbert Meisel, whom I'd met on *Operation Eichmann*. He and Ted Roter, a Belgian writer/director, were preparing to open the Santa Monica Playhouse and wondered if I'd be interested in joining them. The goal was to create a Los Angeles version of the European repertory theater, performing classic, contemporary, and original plays. (We succeeded, by the way. The Santa Monica Playhouse is about to celebrate its fifty-sixth anniversary, and I'm proud to be listed among its founders, along with Ted Roter and James Arness, aka Matt Dillon of *Gunsmoke* fame.)

Our first production, and my first theatrical performance, was a one-act play by Tennessee Williams called *The Lady of Larkspur Lotion,* set in a run-down, roach-infested boardinghouse in New Orleans. I've always been attracted to complex characters, flawed, dark, and conflicted, struggling to make the best of the hand they've been dealt, and Tennessee Williams was a master at creating those characters—in *The Lady of Larkspur Lotion,* for example, I played a writer and raging alcoholic who had a seven-hundred-page manuscript in his desk drawer that he'd been working on for twenty years. (One of my favorite Tennessee Williams quotes, by the way: he was asked for his definition of happiness. His answer was "Insensitivity, I guess.")

I immediately fell in love with performing live onstage and couldn't get enough of it. I next did Jean-Paul Sartre's *Kean,* an existentialist play about Shakespearean actor Edmund Kean that was, to grossly oversimplify it, a study of the interaction between reality and illusion. I played the Prince of Wales, to very flattering reviews for all of us, and the running joke among us actors at the playhouse became, "Today Santa Monica, tomorrow Broadway."

It took a few years, actually, but I got to Broadway, and not alone.

I'd set aside enough money to sign up for some political science and economics classes at Santa Monica College, still very interested in those subjects but still not able to realistically afford pursuing them for any significant length of time.

It was at Santa Monica College that I met a woman named Dale Russell. There was nothing complicated about my initial attraction to her—she had a beautiful face and a beautiful body.

I fell in love with her when I discovered that inside that face and that body were a deep intelligence, an enormous heart, and the soul of an artist. Dale was a graduate of Marymount High, an all-girls Catholic school in Los Angeles. Many of her classmates had grown up in show-business families, so that, in a way, Dale grew up in the business as well and understood it from all angles, from behind the scenes in agencies and executive suites to the spotlight of celebrities like Maureen O'Hara's daughter Bronwyn Fitzsimmons and Maureen O'Sullivan's daughter Mia Farrow.

Incredibly, from the beginning, she also understood me—the actor; the athlete; the competitor; the proud, homesick German; the still-searching, still-unsettled young man. She knew when to encourage me to talk and when to leave me alone. She knew when and how to be supportive and when to call me on my bullshit. She gently led me into an appreciation of art and music and foreign films and color and beauty I would never have taken the time to notice. I was a better man with her in my life, and we began seeing each other on a happy, regular basis. It was Dale who skillfully picked out my Prince of Wales costume for *Kean*, and Dale who was there the night I opened on Broadway.

I'd been doing a lot of episodic television, including an episode of the hit series *Mission: Impossible,* in which I kissed Barbara Bain while playing a Shakespeare-quoting Russian spy. Prolific producer/director George Schaefer happened to see it and flew to L.A. from New York to meet me, which of course was a flattering surprise.

He asked if I'd like to be in a Broadway play he was directing. I was too young and green to fully grasp the significance of what that meant; I just knew I'd enjoyed every minute of being onstage and welcomed the opportunity to do it again. Rather than the euphoric "I'd love to!" he probably expected, I think I responded with nothing more than a quietly excited "Sure."

I was flown to New York to read for the producers onstage at the Eugene O'Neill Theater on Forty-Ninth Street and Broadway. It's common for actors to audition with casting directors as their scene partners, and that audition was no exception. Unfortunately, casting directors are notoriously bad actors. As the scene progressed, the sinking awareness seeped into me that it was a disaster. If I blew that audition, I could deal with it.

But I'd be damned if some flat, wooden casting director was going to blow it for me. So as soon as we finished, I turned to the producers sitting in the audience and said, "Excuse me, would you mind if I do this again?"

They nodded, and we did the scene again. This time I took charge and gave a full-blown performance regardless of what the casting director was or wasn't doing. An hour later the call came to my hotel room—I got the part.

My relationship with Dale had become deep, loving, and very committed. In deference to her Catholic upbringing, we hadn't moved in together, but we'd become inseparable, and at the end of 1965 we were off to Hotel 14 in New York, for rehearsals and three weeks of previews in anticipation of my Broadway debut.

The play was *The Great Indoors,* by Irene Kemp, and the cast was amazing—Geraldine Page, Clarence Williams III, Logan Ramsey, and one of my childhood favorites, Curt Jürgens. Curt Jürgens played a German Jew who'd fled Germany during the Nazi era and come to America to live in the South. My character, his son, stayed in Germany and was then sent to Harvard as an exchange student, a trip during which his mother told him to visit this man (his father) in the South. While there, my character met Clarence's character, Curt's houseboy, and the more the two of them talked, the more convinced they became that they both might be Curt's son.

As written, it was a fascinating play, raising all sorts of interesting questions about identity, and about black/white, German/

Jewish issues. During rehearsals, I admit I became disenchanted with Broadway, as I saw the script go through revisions that, in my opinion, made it more shallow, more commercial, and much less thought provoking. But they hadn't hired me as a critic, they'd hired me to commit to the material I was given and make the most of it, and that's exactly what I set out to do.

It came as no surprise that Curt Jürgens, at six feet four inches, with his long, impressive résumé, was a very commanding presence onstage. I was a bit disappointed to discover that he seemed to feel entitled to that same command offstage. It was our practice to meet with George Schaefer after rehearsals to get George's notes and discuss scenes, and it was Curt's practice to never let anyone complete a sentence without talking over them. We'd all treated him with nothing but respect from the very beginning, and his unwillingness to reciprocate that respect began to infuriate me. Finally one day, when he interrupted me for the third or fourth time, I turned to him and said, "Mr. Jürgens, one moment, please . . . When I've finished speaking, *then* you may continue with what you were saying." He never spoke over me again.

That incident exemplified one of the running themes of my life: no matter what your job, title, or social status, I will regard you with respect, until and unless you fail to do the same for me, at which point, no matter what your job, title, or social status, we're likely to have a problem.

Opening night arrived. February 1, 1966. You could have cut the excitement and nervous tension backstage with a knife.

I wasn't conscious of how frightened I really was until I made the egregious mistake of peeking out at the audience from behind the curtain. In one quick, limited glance, I spotted Tennessee Williams, Lee Strasberg, Mel Brooks, and Anne Bancroft.

I panicked. Oh my God, I couldn't perform in front of those icons. They'd blow my cover. They'd catch on in the blink of an eye that I was an impostor, that I didn't have a clue what I was doing, that I had no business walking across the stage of that Broadway theater, let alone performing on it.

I couldn't do it. I had to get out of there. The stage door was just a few feet away. All I had to do was open it and run.

I literally had my hand on the door handle when an angry "Oh, *hell* no!" flared up inside me. I turned away from the door, marched back to peer out through the tiny split between the curtains at those same people, and silently promised, "I'll be damned if you're going to intimidate me."

I began running up and down the stairs to the dressing rooms and drank some brandy, trying unsuccessfully to get my nervousness under control, but I still had plenty of intensity left over for the performance itself. The exhilarating relief during the bows and applause was a high all its own, a high so satisfying that it made me wonder how I could ever have thought of running away.

We met at the legendary Sardi's later, where, I was told, the patrons applaud as you arrive in accordance with their opinion of your performance. I wasn't accustomed to being greeted by an enthusiastic ovation when I walked into a restaurant, so

I was feeling both flattered and self-conscious as Dale and I joined some of my castmates at a prominent table.

Geraldine Page, such a force of nature onstage, had been especially kind to me from the very beginning. She liked me, she appreciated my talent and my determination to work hard and get it right, and I'm sure she hadn't forgotten the compliment I'd paid her one day while we waited backstage for our cue—that woman had beautiful breasts, and I told her so. She scolded me and warned me against making her husband (Rip Torn) jealous, but she did it with an absolutely beaming smile.

That night at Sardi's she took my hand and led me to a nearby table. Two lovely older women graciously congratulated me on my performance and predicted I had a very successful career ahead of me. I thanked them, told them how nice it was to meet them, and only later found out I'd just been embraced by none other than movie stars Lillian Gish and Viveca Lindfors. I was too new and too overwhelmed by the whole evening to have the slightest idea who all was in that room that night.

Clarence Williams III and I were singled out in glowing reviews by Walter Kerr of the *New York Times* and Stanley Kauffmann of the *New Republic*. Unfortunately, their reviews of *The Great Indoors* in general were fairly dismal, and the play closed after four nights. My disappointment was somewhat mitigated, though, when Geraldine excitedly told me that "Lee Strasberg would love to work with you." Even I had heard of Austrian acting teacher Lee Strasberg, the Method acting guru of the era, who'd coached everyone from James Dean to Paul Newman to Marilyn Monroe to Marlon Brando to Montgomery Clift to director Elia Kazan.

Dale and I briefly extended our stay in New York so that I could sit in on one of his classes. I paid rapt attention, expecting to come away enlightened. Instead, while I'm sure legions of actors would disagree with me, I came away wondering what the fuss was about—all I saw was the performance of a scene by some of the students, followed by the diminutive Strasberg pontificating about it for half an hour without really saying much of anything. I never went back.

I had the opportunity to ask Marlon Brando about Lee Strasberg when we worked together on the film *Morituri* shortly after Dale and I returned to Los Angeles, and it amused me that he claimed he studied with Strasberg for the sole purpose of picking up women.

It goes without saying that Brando was a brilliant, charismatic, extraordinarily powerful actor. He was also a complicated man. We spent a lot of time tossing a football back and forth between scenes on the 20th Century Fox lot where *Morituri* was shot, talking about everything from World War II and the plight of Native Americans to the acting profession.

"Don't be an actor," he said one day. "You're too bright."

It shocked me that a man who'd made such an indelible impact on my generation had so little regard for the craft he'd mastered, that had afforded him legendary status and a lifestyle most people would envy.

Then again, I suppose it was impossible for him to feel gratified by his effect on other people—I've never met anyone, before or since, who cared less what anyone else thought of him. He did exactly what he wanted to do, and he said exactly what he wanted to say, all with a nonnegotiable "take it or leave it" attitude. At first I thought it must be a front, but the more time I spent with him, the more I realized that no, it was utterly authentic, it was who he was, and I must say, I didn't envy him for it.

I was having some serious doubts about committing myself to an acting career at that point, though, which I'm sure is why I took Brando's "you're too bright to be an actor" remark to heart. It wasn't because I felt I was too bright. It was because I couldn't make sense of it.

Hard physical labor made sense to me. Sports made sense to me. Those were the yardsticks I'd used to measure myself and those around me all my life. They were real, they were tangible, and my whole body could feel what I'd accomplished at the end of a long day's work or a tough match. To be well paid and applauded for something so relatively easy, something I enjoyed, something that amounted to nothing more than playacting, almost felt as if I were getting away with something and not carrying my own weight in this world.

I struggled with that inner conflict for another decade or two. But it paled in comparison to a much deeper crisis of the soul I'd been struggling with for the past several years, that had started with a simple trip to the movies.

4

THE SINS OF THE FATHER

It was 1961. Before my first acting job, before Dale, before I had any sense of direction in my life whatsoever. I was in Los Angeles, parking cars at Scandia for a living, and I was terribly homesick. I missed Rosely. I missed my family. I missed Germany. It was all I could do not to pack my bags and head back where I belonged, where my heart was.

A Swedish documentary was playing at a small art house on Wilshire Boulevard. It was called *Mein Kampf (My Struggle).* A film with a German title. Maybe that would help. And it was apparently about Adolf Hitler. We hadn't been taught much about him in school, in deference, I assumed, to all those students whose fathers and brothers had lost their limbs, their health, their minds, or their lives in World War II. I was curious to find out more about this man whose name had come up so often and with such disdain since I'd arrived in America, who'd seemingly become synonymous with Germany itself after only twelve years in power.

I sat down in that dark, virtually deserted theater and walked out two hours later an irrevocably changed man who'd lost his innocence.

Mein Kampf was a graphic, unflinching exposé of the unspeakable atrocities committed against the Jews and all of humanity by a vicious, subhuman, raging megalomaniac named Adolf Hitler and his Nazi Party. All those horrors—stark images of corpses piled like trash in concentration camps, goose-stepping soldiers, Hitler kissing babies, the vile rhetoric of that madman in speeches to tens of thousands of cheering Germans, dead German soldiers standing frozen in the wind, American soldiers liberating walking skeletons from camps—filled me with rage, shame, and deep, profound confusion.

How could my country, a country I loved and in which I'd taken such pride all my life, a country I knew to be filled with good, decent, hardworking people, have allowed this to happen?

Had my own beloved parents and their generation somehow sanctioned this horror? I was just a child when Hitler's reign of terror came to an end, but I was a German child, my father's child, and the sins of the father are indeed visited on the sons. It was unthinkable. But hadn't my own father been taken away by a British officer to be "denazified"?

There was no one around to answer the countless questions swirling in me, or to quiet my deep sense of betrayal. So I began writing letters to my mother, bitter, angry letters demanding explanations and trying to express my indescribable disappointment.

She was an apolitical woman who'd been defiantly against academics since her childhood in a private girls' school. Her life had been too consumed with raising four sons, alone with no money after the sudden death of her husband, to concern herself with politics and other intangible issues she couldn't do a damned thing about. She said it was too complicated to go into in letters but that when I came back to Germany I'd talk to some people who could explain it better than she could. As I read I could almost hear the sigh in her voice that always came when questions simply made her too weary.

It reminded me of an incident that occurred when I was in my early teens. A friend and I were walking into town from school one day when he quietly announced, in what sounded like a confession, that he was Jewish. I asked my mother what it meant—"Jewish" vs. "not Jewish" was a non-issue in our house and among our friends. In fact, I'd never been exposed to even a hint of anti-Semitism or any other prejudice. She'd sighed then too, and added something I didn't understand at the time—"What one did to the white [German] Jews is unforgivable." Looking back, I realized for the first time the gravity of what my friend had confided in me and wondered how he knew so young to be so quiet about it.

I began an intellectual odyssey, determined to educate myself, arm myself with facts, and try to comprehend the incomprehensible. I read everything I could get my hands on about one of the world's two most prolific serial killers and his Nazi henchmen. I talked and listened endlessly. I began to grasp the effectiveness of Hitler's massive propaganda machine—Germany read and heard nothing he didn't want Germany to know. And after the war, the press, and Germans in general, were more consumed with rebuilding their decimated country and their decimated economy than they were with focusing on the Holocaust. As German author and playwright Bertolt Brecht so aptly put it, "Food comes first and then morality." It wasn't until the 1960s, after I'd come to America, that Germany began to openly discuss and deal with the horrors Hitler had unleashed on the Jews and on anyone he even suspected of opposing him.

The more I learned the more impassioned I became, and the more I felt the need to atone on behalf of my country, to find a meaningful way to say, "Germans are not all like that! *I'm* not like that!"

* 500,000 Jews in Germany in 1933 when Hitler came into power, 300,000 of them had left by the late 1930s, while the other 200,000 were among the 11 million human beings who died in concentration camps . . . 6 million of them Jews and more than a million of them children . . .
* Concentration camps originally built to destroy Germans who opposed Hitler and refused to cooperate with the Nazi Party . . .
* 33,000 Jews killed in just two days by German troops at the Babi Yar ravine in the Ukraine, forced to undress and walk to the edge of the ravine, where they were shot to death . . .
* *Kristallnacht,* the "Night of Broken Glass," when 96 Jews were killed and 30,000 arrested in Germany and Austria by Nazis who also burned, looted, and destroyed more than a thousand synagogues and businesses . . .
* More than a million people murdered at Auschwitz alone . . .
* Hitler and the Nazis also targeting the disabled, Gypsies, political and religious opponents, and homosexuals . . .
* In 1938, as Jews tried to flee Europe to escape the Holocaust, thirty-two countries met to discuss the growing refugee crisis, and most of those countries, including Great Britain, Canada, and Australia, refused to offer them asylum. Two boatloads of Jewish refugees were turned away in New York harbor and, with nowhere else to go, were forced to return to Europe . . .

The horrifying list of atrocities went on and on, with no way to process it. My mother had promised we'd talk about all this when we were together, and I intended to take her up on that promise when I was finally able to afford a trip to Germany for Christmas in 1964.

I'd been yearning for five years to see my homeland. I bought a suit and suitcase for the occasion and looked very distinguished, I thought, when a thick fog grounded flights throughout Europe and forced me onto a train from Luxembourg to Germany.

The train station in Hamburg was divided into first, second, and third class, and only third class was open when I arrived at one A.M. The station reeked of smoke and beer, filled to overflowing with local riffraff taking refuge from the cold . . . drunk, loud, and obnoxious. There we were—old soldiers singing Nazi war songs, the broke and homeless singing Christmas songs, and me in my brand-new suit, waiting for my brothers to pick me up, gazing around with bemused chagrin at this crass collection of Germans whose honor I'd been so fiercely defending to anyone who would listen.

My reunion with my family was understandably strained because of the vitriolic letters I'd written to my mother, but there was no less love between us. She still had no answers for me, nor any intention of discussing it. Instead, she invited our neighbor to join us for Christmas dinner.

His name was Christian Röschmann. He was a tough, burly

man whose farm I'd worked on for many years, a man I respected. After dinner he and I sat down alone with some cognac and began to talk. By the time we finished, it was five A.M., and I'd been given a reminder that historical research is incomplete without learning about the human beings who lived that history.

At the age of seventeen, Röschmann was drafted into the Weapons SS, an elite force of the German army, and had fought on the Russian front. He'd seen things and done things while following orders during his service that no one, least of all a boy, should ever experience, things he still relived when he closed his eyes at night, things that would haunt him for the rest of his life. He wept as he reluctantly shared one painful story after another, not wanting sympathy, just working hard day after day since the war, being a good, decent, stoic man and silently praying for absolution.

One of my cousins told me a chilling story I'd never heard before, a story about her father, my uncle Dr. Hans Thomsen, a doctor of jurisprudence, who was married to my mother's sister. It seems that Uncle Hans, part of the intellectual and artistic café society in Hamburg, had been wary of Hitler from the beginning, largely because of the ceremonial book burnings in the 1930s, when the Nazis destroyed books and art they perceived to be subversive or critical of Nazi ideologies. Uncle Hans was extremely well read, preferred the BBC to the propaganda that saturated German radio, and refused to join the Nazi Party, which attracted the Nazis' suspicion.

So one night in 1941, at about two A.M., my uncle, my aunt, and their three daughters were awakened by loud pounding at their front door. It was the Gestapo, demanding to search the house. One of the soldiers quickly spotted a copy of Hitler's book *Mein Kampf* on a nearby table, picked it up and leafed through it, saw my uncle's scornful, satirical notes scrawled in the margins, and said to Uncle Hans, "Pack a suitcase. You're coming with us."

He was imprisoned for a year, until a close friend of his who was an officer in the Wehrmacht (the German army) and had become disillusioned with Hitler, found out about his imprisonment, went to Gestapo headquarters, and demanded Uncle Hans's release.

So much for protesting, even in the privacy of one's own home.

I also spent time with our neighbor Wally Johannssen, who'd been stricken with polio and in a wheelchair since the age of twelve. He was a friend of my father's and told me that in the early 1940s my father had also begun to have serious doubts about Hitler and the Nazi Party.

And my oldest brother remembered that in 1939, when Germany started the war against Poland, our father had shown him a map of Europe to explain why the invasion of Poland was a mistake for Germany and would probably start a second world war, and that he'd once come across two British paratroopers and helped them to safety. In the end, my brother assured me, our father deserved all the admiration we'd given him. I was still confused, still had a million questions I hadn't even begun to think of yet, but I believed him, and was beginning to believe as well that a lot of Germans felt as betrayed by the Nazi regime as I did.

Of course, while I was there, I also saw Rosely.

We'd spent a glorious two weeks together in New York a year earlier, in 1963, when she was there on a trip with her father. I'd flown there for the sole purpose of seeing her for the first time since I'd left Germany. Dale and I had been involved for a couple of years by then, but it wasn't a serious, committed relationship yet—there was no way I could simply dismiss the fact that a large part of my heart still belonged to Rosely, as it had for so long.

Rosely and her father stayed at the St. Regis.

I stayed at a fleabag hotel nearby.

But that didn't stop Rosely from showing up in my room every morning with a basket of fresh fruit for breakfast, loving and cheerful, as if my threadbare little room was exactly where she wanted to be.

Her father wanted to get to know me, so the three of us had lunch at a restaurant in the heart of the financial district. I chose that opportunity, in the mecca of the capitalist world, in the company of a very wealthy German shipping-line magnate, to wax eloquent about Fidel Castro. Rosely reported that once they were alone at the St. Regis again, her father told her, "I was unimpressed with what he said, but I was impressed with how he said it." He felt I should study law and join the family business, which, as the oldest child, Rosely would take over someday.

Before they returned to Germany and I headed back to Los Angeles, Rosely and I talked about getting engaged. I'm sure I knew even then, on that flight from New York to California, that we were approaching an unavoidable impasse and that my future was with Dale; I just wasn't ready to face the finality of me and Rosely yet.

So when we met again for a long walk in 1964, on one of her father's estates in Blankenese, in one of the most affluent neighborhoods in all of Germany, I confessed to her that becoming an attorney for a shipping firm, even *her* shipping firm, was of absolutely no interest to me. My acting career was under way, and while I still hadn't fully committed to it, I had every intention of pursuing it to see where it might lead.

"If you and I are going to proceed with a life together," I explained to her, "you need to come to L.A. with me, live in an apartment, and face the uncertain future of an actor's wife."

She didn't know what to say. Neither did I. I just knew that I would have done us both a great disservice if I'd been less than completely honest.

We agreed to postpone making a final decision about where our relationship was going, but I think we both felt as we said good-bye that the final decision had already been made.

A year later Rosely married a good man named Folkart Schweitzer, who's still her husband today.

I left Germany that Christmas of 1964 looking forward to being with Dale again and ready to commit to her, more at peace with my family and more determined than ever to atone as best I could for the nightmare unleashed against humanity by my beloved country—a process I'd already unintentionally begun.

Come to think of it, 1961 was a very transformative year for me. It was the year I saw *Mein Kampf.* It was the year I stumbled through my first acting job on *Operation Eichmann.* It was the year I met Dale, and it was the year I began to actively pursue sports again, and, almost by accident, found my way onto a soccer team that changed my life.

Sports have been my salvation more times than I can count, particularly when I'm confused and need something to make sense in a world where so few things do. Sports are clear-cut. You win, or you lose. There are rules, and there are consequences if you break them. Sports require fitness, the more the better. They require focus, so being preoccupied with whatever else is going on in your life isn't an option. The physicality of sports relieves stress and is very often the best, least expensive, most immediate therapy to be found.

So it was no coincidence that during my personal journey after seeing *Mein Kampf,* I applied for a track-and-field scholarship at UCLA—too late, as it turned out, so I applied for a soccer scholarship instead. UCLA's soccer coach at the time, a Scotsman named Jock Stewart, told me they didn't give soccer scholarships, but "there's a man in town who pays for players. His name is Jean Leon, and he owns La Scala. You should go have a talk with him."

I'd heard of La Scala, as had almost everyone in Los Angeles. It was one of the most popular restaurants in Beverly Hills. I promptly went there, introduced myself, and found myself talking to a very smart, very successful man who was born and raised in Spain and had an intense passion for soccer. Jean Leon owned a soccer team called the L.A. United, a member of the Greater Los Angeles Soccer League, and the team's manager was Dan Tana, owner of another popular restaurant in Beverly Hills that bore his name. Jean Leon made it clear from the moment we met that his ultimate goal was to put together the best soccer team in America, and he invited me to come to an L.A. United practice on Tuesday night.

Practice was held at a park on La Cienega between Wilshire and Olympic, where I found myself surrounded by some of the top players in the world—England's top division players Billy Steele, Roy Milne, Paddy Ratcliffe, National Hall of Famer Albert Zerhusen, and many, many more. I played with them and was immediately signed to the team, for a paycheck of ten dollars a game, with the added bonus of an offer to work as a busboy at La Scala. I accepted on the only-half-kidding condition that I be assigned tables close to the kitchen, since I was always hungry and wanted as much food as possible within easy reach. Scheduling around auditions and acting jobs wasn't a problem—I think every restaurant owner in this city is aware that many of their hires are aspiring actors, and they adjust accordingly.

Most of the La Scala service staff were Latins, and those who weren't teammates were soccer fans and attended every game. A fellow busboy was also our Yugoslavian goalkeeper; he and I painted the bathrooms and windowsills at another of Jean Leon's restaurants, Au Petit Jean, across the street from La Scala. At work and on the soccer field, I was happily surrounded by expatriates, one of whom remains my best friend to this day.

Michael Meyer and I met playing for the L.A. United team. He'd been a star soccer player at UCLA, and our mutual love of the game was only the beginning of all we had in common. We were both from German villages. Both our fathers were mayor of those villages. We both had three brothers, and we were both immersed in learning everything there was to know about the Nazi period in Germany, although Mike's life during that era had been far more directly affected than mine. He'd been hidden from the Nazis by his father's family during the war, unaware until he was in his teens that his mother was Jewish, and many of his mother's relatives died in concentration camps. It's no surprise that Mike went on to become a professor of European intellectual history with an emphasis on the

Nazi period at California State University in Northridge, and that we developed a deep and enduring friendship.

L.A. United played our games on Sundays at a field that was then called Rancho Cienega but is now the Jackie Robinson Stadium. Anywhere from three to five thousand people would come to watch, not one of them American. Our opponents were first-division players from all over the world—England, Wales, Scotland, Germany, Denmark, Uruguay, Mexico, Peru, Chile, you name it—and we used to joke that once a week we were fighting the First and Second World Wars all over again on that Rancho Cienega soccer field.

Jean Leon did overreach for one game, when he invited the brilliant Spanish team Real Madrid to come play. Real Madrid was *the* team, with players like Alfredo Di Stéfano and Ferenc Puskás, and we were proud that they accepted the invitation, but it was a bit like a sandlot team in Burbank taking on the New York Yankees. That particular game was played in the Los Angeles Coliseum, to a huge crowd, and we lost 9–0. The experience was worth it, though, and Jean Leon threw a forty-thousand-dollar party for both teams at La Scala that night.

A Hungarian Jew named Joe Schwartz carried the buckets for L.A. United. He'd been openly impressed with Mike's and my soccer skills, and one day he approached us and asked if we'd be interested in playing for a team called the Maccabees. We liked Joe and respected him, and we said yes. We went to a practice and joined the team and quickly became aware that the Maccabees was a Jewish team. Two German guys, playing side by side with people who'd suffered at the hands of the Nazi regime? An opportunity for me to do something I loved and atone for the "sins of the fathers" at the same time? Hell, yes!

That's yet another thing I love about sports—the team welcomed us two German guys without a hint of apprehension or reluctance. Both on and off the field, all that mattered was that we were on the same team, playing and supporting each other for the common goal of winning, and race, religion, and nationality were completely beside the point.

The coach of the Maccabees, Max Wosniak, was one of my greatest teachers and inspirations in both soccer and basic human decency. He was a German Jew who'd been thrown out of Germany at the age of twelve and sent first to Poland and then to Russia. Despite a childhood of terrible experiences, he became a spectacular athlete and devoted his life to soccer. He returned to Poland after the war and played in their first division as a champion goalkeeper. He moved on to the first division in Israel, where his career as a player was interrupted by a broken leg. From there he returned to Germany in the late 1950s, graduated from the German Sport University Cologne, got his coaching license, and then became a goalie for the first-division German team until finding his way to the Maccabees. It was an honor to know him and play for him.

Eventually our team included seven Israelis, two Ethiopians, several Brazilians, and an Argentinian goalkeeper, and still, from time to time, prejudice would rear its ugly head on the field. We were playing a Croatian team one Sunday afternoon when I tackled one of their biggest, brawniest players. He rose to his feet and growled at me, "You fucking Nazi, you fucking Jew!" I growled back the only possible response: "Which is it, you moron?"

I was becoming more and more sensitized to prejudice as those years went along—not just against Jews but against any race or nationality. I thought back to those segregated water fountains in bus stations on my trip from New York to Galveston. I thought back to 1959 and the one black player on the University of Montana football team who wasn't allowed into the same bars where his teammates celebrated after a winning game. What I'd found mystifying back then began to outrage me in the early 1960s, when I began to pay attention to how pervasive bigotry really is, among even the people who are purportedly the most sophisticated—it was stated to me as common knowledge, for example, that two of Hollywood's most exclusive hot spots, the Jonathan Club and the Los Angeles Country Club, didn't accept Jews into their memberships.

I started asking the same questions of bigots I'm still asking today: Did any of us choose who our parents were, or what race they were, or in what country we were born? Of course not. So how can we possibly feel superior to anyone based on aspects of ourselves we had nothing to do with? It's insane to me.

I only left the Maccabees when, at the age of thirty-two, I

was considering an offer to play for the National Soccer League and noticed during a game that I'd become a step slower on the field. My teammates and I were accustomed to a high quality of athleticism from me, and if I couldn't measure up to that quality anymore, I couldn't in good conscience continue to play at that level. I was sad to retire from semiprofessional soccer, but it was time.

Some of my teammates and I formed friendships that have lasted to this day. Israelis Benny Bienenstock (incidentally, the toughest player I've ever known), Moishe Hoffman, Mike Shapov, Eli Namour, Chaim Gonsharov, Pini Ben Bassad, Jumbo Cohen, Jerry Schnitman, an Ethiopian named Fessah, and, of course, my best friend, Mike Meyer, and I still get together on Tuesday nights to catch up on each other's lives and compare physical ailments.

I wouldn't trade my ten years with the Maccabees for anything on earth. One of the proudest, most satisfying experiences of my life was that day in 1973 when we won the National Soccer Championship, defeating the Cleveland Inter Italians 5–3. I, by the way, scored the first goal of the game.

And one of the most abiding memories from my years with the Maccabees was that era in which I proudly wore the Star of David on my soccer jersey on weekends, and during the week, practiced with some of my teammates at the studio, kicking a soccer ball around in my Nazi boots between scenes of a series called *The Rat Patrol*.

I'd been asked by writer/director Tom Gries if I'd be interested in playing a German soldier in a television series about the Rommel campaign in North Africa during World War II.

I was immediately skeptical. Hollywood had already done more than enough projects that vilified Germany and implied that "German" and "Nazi" were synonyms, especially when it came to soldiers, and I wanted nothing to do with portraying yet another ideologically convinced Nazi.

Tom assured me that my character, Captain Hans Dietrich, was being written as a "normal" man who was simply serving his country. He'd be a smart, worthy nemesis for the Rat Patrol, but with a sense of honor and a humanity that set him apart from his Nazi counterparts in the German army, even though they wore the same uniforms and the same tall pain-in-the-ass boots.

An opportunity to play a decent, honorable German officer? Yes, I was very interested, and we were off to Yuma, Arizona to shoot the pilot. ABC gave us the green light to proceed with the series, and *The Rat Patrol* began its two-year run, from 1966 to 1968.

We shot the first sixteen episodes in Spain. "Cheaper," the suits said, although we cast members always wondered if there might be some behind-the-scenes skimming going on. Almería, Spain was the location, so that's where we went, and we left the financial improprieties, if there were any, to the forensic accountants.

Dale and I arrived in Madrid and took a train to Almería in a thunderstorm on a pitch-black night. We were picked up by horse and buggy and taken to our hotel, where we encountered evidence that this wasn't a region of Spain that had been supportive of dictator Francisco Franco. It was an area that had offered resistance to him and, as a result, had been deprived of governmental financial assistance and privileges and was suffering from neglect.

Our run-down hotel leaned slightly, so the elevators routinely got stuck between floors.

I found a cockroach doing a leisurely breaststroke in my soup at one of Almería's nicer restaurants.

We were moved to an apartment building owned by a Hungarian count, on the shores of the Mediterranean. I loved waking up in the morning and jumping into the sea for a swim, until I looked up one day to find feces floating toward me, thanks to the town's pathetically outdated sewer system.

Through it all, Dale, a Europhile to her core, able to see beauty where I focused on feces and cockroaches, found Spain to be one of the most romantic countries she'd ever seen and continues to cherish her memories of it, despite Francisco Franco, and despite me . . .

My younger brother Jochen came to visit us in Spain, and he and Dale and I decided to make the drive from Almería to Marbella, several hours away along the Mediterranean coast. I so resented the exorbitant cost of the rental car that I remember promising the man behind the counter that by the time that car came back, there would be a whole lot wrong with it.

The road was serpentine, with crosses at many of the sharp curves in memory of people who'd crashed and died there. It was probably beautifully scenic, and Dale would have loved every detail of the landscape, every wave of the sea, if I'd given her the opportunity.

Unfortunately, there was a MINI Cooper ahead of us whose driver clearly wanted to race, and far be it from me to back off from a challenge when I'm behind the wheel. In an instant, all thoughts of Dale's sensibilities and my brother's comfort in the backseat vanished and tunnel vision took over—I'd be damned if that MINI Cooper was going to beat me to Marbella. It took every ounce of skill and concentration I could muster, for the hours it took to accomplish it, but it was exhilarating as hell.

I won.

And so what?

Only after the fact did it hit me that I'd just treated Dale to those same hours of clinging to her door handle for dear life, and my brother to those same hours of bracing himself behind her with his eyes closed, praying to survive.

I still regret it. I've apologized to Dale many times, and she's forgiven me over and over again. It's one of those days I wish I could do over, with the added bonus of some maturity and thoughtfulness. I would handle it so differently . . . I hope . . .

When I finally slowed down and started looking past the

cockroaches and the prehistoric Almería sewer system, I enjoyed Spain very much, from the picturesque countryside to the fascinating diversity of its architecture and its people. On the set of *The Rat Patrol* we were usually surrounded by extras from the Spanish army, who were paid a dollar a day for their time. Off the set, between scenes, my new Spanish and Gypsy friends and I would play soccer, possibly Spain's most beloved sport, some of them in their army uniforms, some of them in their street clothes, and me in my stern German officer wardrobe and Nazi boots.

I tried discussing politics with them and asking about their lives under Franco's rule. They'd immediately stop talking or quickly change the subject, not knowing who might be listening and report back to a government they'd learned not to trust.

We had an exemplary cast on *The Rat Patrol,* and a hardworking crew who overcame a lot of obstacles with a lot of expertise, swearing, and more patience than I would have had—almost daily we'd lose hours of production time because a piece of outdated equipment took its last breath or our power supply inexplicably went down.

Our ratings were very high when the series debuted on ABC. The network only had one complaint after seven or eight episodes had aired. It seems the audience was finding my character, Captain Dietrich, "too sympathetic." So the suits in Los Angeles sent word to the producers in Spain, delivered to me by our production manager Fred Lemoine, that from our current episode forward, they'd like me to play Dietrich with an eye patch and a limp.

"Ain't gonna happen," I told him.

The Rat Patrol, with all due respect to Tom Gries and our cast and crew, already felt like a bit of a cartoon to me. Essentially, it implied, week after week, that these four Allied guys in a couple of Jeeps were able to defeat the tanks and expertise of a German panzer division. And despite the fact that they were fighting for the wrong cause in World War II, the German army happened to be among the best on earth. The thought of contributing to that nonsense by reducing Captain Dietrich to a stereotypical heel-clicking Nazi idiot was out of the question. I would have walked away without a single regret before I'd have let that happen.

In the end, I kept right on playing Dietrich as the character I'd been attracted to in the first place, a human being caught up in the machinery of war who did what was expected of him, in conflict with a deep sense of morality he had to play close to his chest in order to keep his job.

After sixteen episodes, *The Rat Patrol* moved back to Los Angeles, to the MGM studios and the Mojave Desert.

But before we left Europe, Dale and I stopped in Paris, arguably Dale's favorite city in the world, to visit my cousin Rita, the youngest of Uncle Hans Thomsen's daughters. It was Rita's two sisters who were so helpful to me when I first arrived in America, and the three of them have always been very important to me and my family.

Rita was a tall, regal northern German lady, fifteen years my senior, incredibly gracious and bright. She was studying music in Paris and was friends with the likes of Jean-Paul Sartre and Albert Camus and Simone de Beauvoir. She and her husband Edmund took us to restaurants like Café de Flore and Les Deux Magots on the Left Bank, where Hemingway and Picasso loved to eat and create, where Sartre and a wealth of other existentialists used to hang out in the 1960s and exchange ideas for hours on end. It was easy to picture them there, and the air itself felt so alive and stimulating that you found yourself almost expecting them to walk through the doors at any moment and sit down at the table beside you. The soft lavender light of Parisian afternoons, the rare light some Impressionists have captured so specifically, the light I might never have taken the time to notice if Dale hadn't called my attention to it, made our trip there seem almost like an artist's rendering itself. It was a visit Dale and I still treasure and will never forget.

From there it was off to Germany, to take care of two very pleasant pieces of business—to introduce Dale to my mother and brothers, and now that I could finally afford it, to fulfill the longtime dream of buying my mother a house.

My family was happy and excited for me that the acting career none of us saw coming was showing signs of success. They hadn't seen any of my work, celebrity didn't impress them in the least, and they couldn't begin to relate to what I was doing for a living. Nor did I blame them—I was still struggling to relate to it myself. But the joyful disbelief on my mother's face when

I told her I was buying her a house is a look I carry with me to this day, and it was a privilege, such a small gesture in exchange for the extraordinary love, courage, dignity, and patience with which she'd raised my brothers and me.

Their introduction to Dale went as beautifully as I knew it would. They immediately responded to her fundamental sweetness, and she liked them every bit as much as they liked her. The only slight awkwardness was the language barrier. I spent the entire visit translating even the most casual conversations between them from German to English and English to German, which was a bit exhausting. But as these sometimes strained meeting-the-family formalities go, it was an absolute pleasure.

And then, finally, it was time to return to L.A., where I was very much looking forward to reuniting with the Maccabees, to playing soccer at the studio between scenes with my teammates in my Nazi boots again, and to beginning my life as a married man.

5

BECOMING ERIC BRAEDEN

On October 8, 1966, Dale and I were married in a beautiful old house in Flintridge that belonged to her mother and stepfather. There were twelve of us in attendance, including my best man, Mike Meyer, and his wife, Miriam; Dale's sister, who was her maid of honor; and the rest of her immediate family. We'd only made the decision a few weeks earlier, which wasn't enough notice for my mother and brothers to travel from Germany, but I knew that after meeting Dale and seeing how happy she and I were together, they were cheering us on.

A few months later, before we resumed production of *The Rat Patrol* in California, I fulfilled another long-standing dream—I bought myself a Porsche 911 Targa, in classic racing green. Tom Gries cosigned for me, and I enjoyed that car so much that I managed to get five speeding tickets in six months, the last one, I was convinced, for no other reason than that I was driving a Porsche.

I wasn't about to pay that last ticket without a fight. My court date happened to fall on a day when I was working, so the assistant director scheduled around me as best he could, but insisted that I "be back in two hours."

Two hours left me no time to spare, not even time to change into my street clothes, so I walked into that courtroom in full wardrobe, Nazi boots and all, my cap under my arm. Some of the cops in attendance were apparently *Rat Patrol* fans and were nudging each other and grinning from ear to ear as my case was called.

I'd decided to represent myself, armed with a question a friend suggested for the patrolman who'd pulled me over. When the time came I pulled that question out of my hip pocket:

"Officer, when is the last time your speedometer was calibrated?"

The officer had no idea.

Case dismissed.

It was a very satisfying moment, but it didn't address the bigger, more inescapable issue that my Porsche Targa and I as a team simply weren't capable of adhering to posted speed-limit signs. At what I'll politely call Dale's enthusiastic, repeated encourageement, I sadly traded it in for a car with which she'd fallen hopelessly in love—a 1953 right-hand-drive Bentley. It was a handsome car, not especially reliable mechanically and certainly not conducive to darting deftly around in L.A. traffic, but it did improve my driving record. I hated that car.

The two-year run of *The Rat Patrol* had barely ended when Tom Gries approached me about his next project, an action film he was writing and directing called *100 Rifles*. It was a story set in early-twentieth-century Mexico and involved an Arizona lawman in search of a bank robber who stole six thousand dollars to buy a hundred rifles for his oppressed Yaqui Indian people.

I'd be playing the role of German military advisor Lieutenant Von Klemme. The rest of the cast included Burt Reynolds, Raquel Welch, Fernando Lamas, Dan O'Herlihy, and the newly retired Cleveland Browns' superstar fullback Jim Brown.

It meant a return to those damned German military boots. It also meant a chance to work with my friend Tom Gries again, and a return to Spain.

Count me in.

Tom, our producer Marvin Schwartz, the cast, Dale, and I gathered for our first dinner together at a new hotel in Aguadulce, a farm village a bit east of Almería. We ate poolside in the soft air of a warm Spanish night. Raquel was with her husband, Patrick Curtis; Dan's wife was at home in the U.S. with their four children; Burt and Jim's significant others hadn't arrived yet; and Fernando joked that his wife, Esther Williams, would be along as soon as she finished swimming the Straits of Gibraltar. I was drawn to his sense of humor immediately and looked forward to getting to know him.

It was 1968, and the dinner conversation inevitably evolved into discussions about civil rights and the Vietnam War. Things were rolling along smoothly until Raquel made a well-intentioned effort to contribute some profound, liberal observation about civil rights. I don't remember what it was, but I distinctly remember Jim Brown's response—he aimed a bone-chilling glare at her and said, "You don't know what the hell you're talking about."

That pretty much set the tone for our two romantic leads, and for the film itself.

I read a quote by Burt Reynolds after *100 Rifles* was released that offered his perspective on the odd out-of-synch undercurrent that showed up on the screen: "I was playing Yaqui Joe, supposedly an Indian with a mustache. Raquel had a Spanish accent that sounded like a cross between Carmen Miranda and Zasu Pitts. Jimmy Brown was afraid of only two things in the entire world. One was heights, the other was horses. And he was on a horse fighting me on a cliff. It just didn't work."

While *100 Rifles* didn't exactly ignite a stampede at the box office, the location shoot was one I'll always remember, for a number of reasons.

I enjoyed getting acquainted with Jim Brown, with whom

I had many interesting discussions on a variety of issues. I've never been one to adjust my opinions based on whom I'm talking to, so while we didn't always see eye to eye in those conversations, he knew he was getting nothing but honesty from me and an enormous amount of respect. *Ebony* magazine came to interview him on the set one day, and after they talked, the reporter commented to me, "You know, you're the only white guy who's ever talked back to Jim Brown."

Dan O'Herlihy, a veteran actor whose work I'd always admired, turned out to be a very nice, very intelligent, very well-read man as well, and on weekends, when we'd all gather to relax by the pool, he and I would share our mutual interest in history and politics.

I greatly admired Burt Reynolds for doing all his own stunts, and I made a point of being on the set the day they shot a scene in which five-foot, eleven-inch, 180-pound Burt Reynolds was supposed to tackle six-foot, two-inch, 235-pound Jim Brown. It required several takes before Burt stopped bouncing off of Jim's back like a Chihuahua trying to take down a bull mastiff.

I had my own very satisfying encounter with a stuntman. My character was spearheading a charge by a group of Mexican horsemen, and when the stuntman brought me my horse, I paused before mounting it, sensing a possible problem, and said, "It seems skittish." The stuntman decided to argue about it, dismissively insisting there was nothing skittish about that horse. Finally, tired of discussing it, I told him, "Then *you* get on it." He did, and the horse promptly threw him. The stuntman didn't find it nearly as funny as I did.

The production moved to Granada, with its extraordinary blend of Moorish and medieval Catholic architecture and a palpable sense of history and suffering and courage in the air. We stayed at a hotel across from the Alhambra, a magnificent palace and fortress that was renovated into its current form in the thirteenth century, a breathtaking testament to the very height of Moorish civilization. The Alhambra was set against a backdrop of mountains, and at night we could see fires in the hillside caves where the Gypsies lived, and hear their distant songs. Dale and I spent hours finding treasures at the many local antiques stores, and two pieces of furniture in our home today were shipped from Granada. It took them six months to arrive, but it was worth the wait.

I had the pleasure of reviving my Spanish tradition of playing soccer with the Gypsies between scenes in yet another pair of tall German military boots, and one day they honored Dale and me with an invitation to visit their caves that night after all the tourists had left. It was an unforgettable evening, sitting at a long, simple table surrounded by whitewashed walls while our hosts entertained us with improvised songs about us, and the beauty of Dale's eyes, a cappella, using the table for percussion. We felt transported to a time centuries ago, and we soaked up the magic of it like sponges.

Dale loved shopping, sightseeing, and taking pictures in

Almería, but she started coming to me with stories about the perpetual aggression she was dealing with from Spanish men. At least in that era of Spain's history, attractive foreign women seemed to be regarded as whores, and gangs of men felt perfectly entitled to follow them, accompanying themselves with loud, rude, obscene catcalls and sound effects. Dale, sometimes with Raquel and sometimes by herself, would be walking down the street, conservatively dressed, only to find a growing crowd of obnoxious macho bullies pursuing her.

One day when she was alone and scared and an aggressive gang was so close behind her they were stepping on the heels of her shoes, she decided she'd had it, and her only hope was to gain some psychological advantage by doing the last thing these men would expect. She suddenly turned on them, began swinging her beloved German camera at them by its shoulder strap, and cursing at them in Spanish at the top of her lungs, thanks to the extensive vocabulary of vile epithets she'd learned from the *100 Rifles* crew. Sure enough, the men, completely shocked, turned and ran. Incredibly, moments later an English-speaking foreigner who'd witnessed the whole thing stepped up to her and warned her not to do that again. "You'll be arrested," she was told. "You're not Spanish."

On another occasion she was walking along in a fairly deserted area of Almería and realized a carload of these thugs was following her. This time she made good use of the fact that Spain was profoundly Catholic: she stopped, fell to her knees, pulled out a rosary she was carrying in case a situation like this came up, and began praying in broken Spanish. She turned to the men who'd emerged from their car and were assembling around her and said, "Mother of God does not want you to do this," upon which they turned away, retreated to their car, and drove off.

I found these stories incredible. It wasn't that I doubted my wife; I just couldn't fathom this behavior. A group of men whistling, yelling, and making idiots of themselves when a gorgeous woman or two walked by was no surprise, but chasing them down like a pack of hyenas in broad daylight was unimaginable to me. So I took Dale up on her challenge to go with her and see for myself.

I stayed several yards behind her as she walked along a well-populated commercial street. She was modestly dressed, window-shopping and minding her own business, and I'll be damned, within just a few short blocks, seven or eight guys were closing in on her like moths to a flame, with more on the way.

I quickly caught up with her and squared off with these appalling assholes. I was bigger and in much better shape than they were, and the look on my face clearly transcended all language barriers with the message "Leave her alone or deal with me. Those are your choices."

Like all other bullies, they were cowards and promptly disappeared.

I'd never seen such a reprehensible example of crowd mentality aimed at a woman before, and I hope to never see it again.

The production took a week off, and Tom Gries offered his huge flat in Madrid to Fernando, Esther, Dale, and me. Dale and I had grown enormously fond of Fernando and Esther—Esther Williams was a fun-loving woman, and Fernando Lamas was a gentleman with an utterly delightful sense of humor. The four of us shared some wonderful meals together at Casa Botín, the world's oldest restaurant and Ernest Hemingway's favorite haunt in Madrid. Dale pointed out the Spanish aristocracy who would arrive late at night for dinner at Madrid's most expensive restaurants, sometime between ten and midnight, and how much they looked like Goya paintings, with white faces and aquiline noses, fascinating faces etched with history.

As luck would have it, the Spanish Cup final was being played that week at Real Madrid's home stadium, the Estadio Santiago Bernabéu, a match between Spain's archrivals, Real Madrid and Barcelona, so I seized the opportunity to introduce Burt and Jim to the game of soccer.

We'd just parked our car and were walking to the stadium when we heard an approaching roar in the street and turned to see a cavalcade of BMW motorcycles headed toward us, their uniformed riders armed with machine guns strapped across their backs. Directly behind them were two Cadillac convertibles, tops down and filled with more heavily armed soldiers/bodyguards. Next came two Rolls-Royces with heavily tinted windows, and by that time it was apparent what was going on—one of the Rolls-Royces was a decoy, while the other was transporting dictator Francisco Franco himself, all five feet four inches of him. Bringing up the rear was another cavalcade of BMW motorcycles. It was quite a spectacle, a clear signal to the people of Spain that Franco was in charge and there was every reason to be afraid.

Our seats were at the top of the stadium, so we had a clear view of the moment when Franco and his entourage arrived. The instant they sat down, the huge crowd erupted in wild applause—not for him, I insisted on believing, but because finally the game could begin.

By the way, in case you're wondering, Barcelona beat Real Madrid 1–0 to win the Spanish Cup.

It was in Tom Gries's flat in Madrid that I received a call from my agent, Alex Brewis. He'd been determined to find a role for me in which I could finally play something other than a German military officer/Nazi, as if I weren't even more sick of it than he was, and he had potentially good news.

"Universal Studios wants to see you for the lead in a film. Can you fly to Los Angeles right away for a screen test and then fly back to Spain again?" The lead, he went on to tell me, was an American scientist, and I tried to imagine the luxury of a wardrobe that didn't involve stiff black knee-high boots.

The timing was perfect, and I was on a plane to L.A. the next day. I did the screen test at Universal and returned to Spain excited but trying not to get my hopes up too high in case it didn't work out.

The call came to the Madrid apartment three days later—I

got the job! I was going to star in a movie for Universal Studios! I nearly jumped through the ceiling.

After a brief pause, Alex added, "But . . ."

Why does there always have to be a "but"?

It seems that Lew Wasserman, the powerful head of Universal, had added a condition to the offer: The job was mine if, and only if, I changed my name. "No one with a German name is going to star in an American picture," Wasserman said, and Hans Gudegast was most certainly a German name.

As decisions go, that one was easy. "Tell Lew Wasserman to go fuck himself," I shot back, and hung up the phone. Being asked to change my name felt like being asked to apologize for who I was and where I was from, and I'd be damned if I would ever let that happen, nor would I ever run the risk of offending my family. Besides, I'd been working very hard to build a career as Hans Gudegast. Was I supposed to let all that hard work go to waste by essentially declaring that Hans Gudegast no longer existed?

Dale wisely left me alone for a while to rage and vent and detonate before I calmed down enough to be reasoned with. She would be supportive of any decision I made, as always, she assured me, but she was much smarter about the industry than I was, so she wisely pointed out that I was taking Lew Wasserman's business decision much too personally. What hit closest to home, though, was her reminding me of a conversation I'd had a few years earlier.

"When you were doing *The Great Indoors* on Broadway,

Curt Jürgens told you that as a German actor in America, you'd never play anything but Nazis. You've always wanted to prove him wrong. Here's your opportunity. Are you really going to pass it up?"

I was mulling all this over when Joe Behm, our *100 Rifles* unit production manager, called to say that Fernando and I were needed back in Almería immediately. I was convinced that Behm harbored a contempt for actors in general, as if we were nothing more than occupational inconveniences in his life, and I didn't appreciate his tone. We were obviously in Madrid with Tom Gries's full permission, even staying in his apartment, but Behm's exasperation implied that we'd been hiding out playing hooky like disobedient children and inconveniencing the rest of the cast and crew by our absence.

He'd arranged transportation to Almería, he barked, and we were to proceed to the airport ASAP and follow instructions from there.

Next thing we knew, Dale; Fernando; Esther; their eleven-year-old son, Lorenzo; and I were crammed into a rickety mail plane, bouncing and sputtering our way back to work, undoubtedly exceeding the small aircraft's maximum weight allowance. The closest I've ever come to death was on that trip, when we came within inches of colliding with the Sierra Nevada mountains. It terrified all of us, and I was seething by the time Fernando and I arrived on the set and Behm made the unfortunate choice of greeting us with an enraged "You guys will never work in this town again!"

I don't think I even bothered to raise my voice when I stepped up to him, almost but not quite touching him, and promised, "If I ever hear one word against either of us that came from you, I'll come looking for you, and I will find you."

Behm went slinking off before the rest of the blood could drain from his face, while Fernando turned to me with the concern of a friend.

"Are you sure you should talk to him like that?"

"Are you kidding?" I said. "I'll be damned if I'm going to take that shit from him or anyone else."

Fernando, who was one the most professional, conscientious actors I've ever known, had been scolded repeatedly by Joe Behm for being late to the set, all due to Almería's still-prehistoric public transportation system. I watched with great satisfaction as he squared his shoulders, marched onto the set, and gave Behm, the producers, and everyone else within earshot one hell of an eloquent, long-overdue lecture on the potential downside of treating a hardworking cast and crew with anything less than the respect they deserve.

We were never subjected to another scolding from Joe Behm.

Once we were all back to work, I talked to Tom Gries and a few of my castmates about my name-change dilemma, and I was grateful when they helped put it in a little more perspective by making me laugh with some very funny alternative-name ideas. Finally, after one more soul-searching conversation with Dale, I made the difficult decision that, all right, for purely professional reasons, I would change my name, provided it was a name I could connect with emotionally.

"Eric" was a common Northern European name, so I'd be comfortable with that.

"Braeden" would be a way to honor my hometown of Bredenbek, with the addition of the *a* to keep the pronunciation accurate—without the *a,* it would have been pronounced "BREE-den," a name that would mean nothing to me.

After some long, deep breaths, I called my agent, who'd been wise enough not to pass along my anatomically unlikely suggestion to Lew Wasserman that he go fuck himself and simply wait me out before responding to the Universal offer.

And so it was that I began my career as Eric Braeden, in a movie called *Colossus: The Forbin Project.*

But first, as soon as the *100 Rifles* shoot ended, with a little time off before *Colossus* filming began, Dale and I headed off for a visit with my mother and brothers and then on to a further exploration of Europe before we flew back to the United States. We rented a car in Germany, drove to exquisite Geneva, and spent the night at an equally exquisite hotel, then left the next morning for our ultimate destination in the south of France.

I asked the concierge how long it would take us to drive from Geneva to Cannes by way of the historic Route Napoléon, which we both wanted to see. I don't remember his exact answer, but let's say it was eight hours. Sadly, I was still afflicted with the same involuntary competitive impulse when it came to driving that had sent us hurtling across Spain during the filming of *The Rat Patrol.* I heard, "It takes eight hours," and immediately thought, "I'll do it in seven and a half." I was putting on my invisible fire suit and crash helmet as we walked to our rented Mercedes, and the Route Napoléon had now become, in my mind, the Daytona 500 speedway.

So off we flew along the same extraordinary route of Napoléon's legendary march from Elba to Grenoble in 1815, my patient Europhile wife not interjecting a word of complaint about experiencing the magnificent scenery as a blur. In my defense, I did occasionally pull over so we could leap out of the car and take a few pictures before speeding on to our destination. I'm sure we beat the eight-hour time limit. In retrospect, it wasn't worth it. And to further confirm that Dale would remember that particular leg of our European vacation for all the wrong reasons, it turned out that the film in my camera was defective, so that not a single picture I took along the Route Napoléon came out.

We managed to arrive safely in Juan-les-Pin in the south of France during a beautiful summer dusk, and we began looking for a place to stay. One of the many hotels in Juan-les-Pin, a magnificent structure called the Hotel du Cap, took Dale's breath away. "Oh my God," she said, "can we stay there?" But I took one look at the Ferraris, Rolls-Royces, and Maseratis lined up at the entrance, told her it was too expensive, and drove on to settle into more affordable lodging for the night.

The next morning we headed on to Saint-Tropez. The narrow streets were so clogged with traffic that it made the Pacific Coast Highway seem deserted by comparison, and I wasn't a good sport about inching our way along. But we'd arranged to meet Rosely and her husband at one of her father's hotels, so turning back was not an option.

Rosely and I had kept in touch over the years. We were well aware that we'd both moved on, and we'd settled into an enduring, appropriate fondness for each other that was no threat to either of our marriages. What could otherwise have been an awkward situation was nothing but cordial and comfortable. It was wonderful to see her again, and she and Dale thoroughly enjoyed each other. We were meeting Rosely's husband Folkart for the first time, and they seemed happy together, exactly as I wished for her. In fact, not long ago, Rosely and Folkart visited Dale and me at our Los Angeles home, almost sixty years after that house party in Rendsburg where Rosely and I first danced and fell in love.

I still remember the first moments of that reunion in Saint-Tropez as Dale and I described our trip from Geneva the day before.

Rosely asked where we stayed in Juan-les-Pin. I told her.

"Oh," she replied, sorry to hear it, "you should have stayed at Daddy's hotel."

"Daddy's hotel," of course, turned out to be the Hotel du Cap.

That afternoon the four of us proceeded to the beach, where I noticed an impromptu soccer game going on not far away. I was at the height of my soccer career and couldn't resist approaching them. There were five players, obviously of the highest level, and I asked if they'd like a sixth player, juggling the ball a bit to show them I wasn't a novice. They turned out to be players from Ajax Amsterdam, one of the finest teams in the world, on summer vacation. We played beach soccer, which is exhausting, and it was truly a joy for me that I won't forget.

And then, finally, after several days of relaxing and playing soccer on the beaches in the south of France, it was time to return to Los Angeles, excited to begin shooting *Colossus: The Forbin Project.*

Colossus was the name of a highly advanced computer designed by my character, Dr. Charles Forbin, to control America's nuclear defense system. Once it was up and running, Colossus discovered the existence of its Russian counterpart, Guardian. The two computers linked into one supercomputer that threatened the total nuclear destruction of the planet if the link was broken, and then began making plans to take over the world while Forbin and his colleagues worked frantically to disarm the monster they'd created.

I'll be the first to admit that the subject matter didn't interest me any more than computers interest me now, but I liked the prescient concept and I thoroughly enjoyed shooting the film. The set on Stage 12 at Universal Studios was fantastic, and we had a terrific cast that included Susan Clark, William Schallert, Gordon Pinsent, and Georg Stanford Brown, who became a good friend.

I especially loved working with our director, Joseph Sargent. It's been my experience that the best directors are former actors, or have at least studied acting. Otherwise, too many of them are little more than traffic cops. Joe was a former actor, and he was wonderful.

We had a frequent visitor to the set who came to observe—and by the way, a visitor who's proved to be a glaring exception to my actor/director experience—a young upstart named Steven Spielberg, newly under contract to Universal. He was so smart, so respectful and enthusiastic and refreshingly down to earth, that his massive success comes as no surprise.

And of course, a return to Los Angeles meant a long-awaited reunion with the Maccabees—practicing three nights a week with my teammates and friends again, games on Sundays and playing soccer with them on the lot between scenes, felt like home and helped keep me grounded at a time when I really needed it.

I'VE COME TO BELIEVE THAT ALL AGENTS SHOULD PRESENT their clients with the names and numbers of therapists who can help actors navigate the highs and lows of success.

This is a small town and a small business, and between *Vari-*

ety and the *Hollywood Reporter* and talent agencies and dinners at popular restaurants like the Musso & Frank Grill, La Scala, Dan Tana's, and the Bistro, word of who's "in" and who's "out" spreads quickly.

I had the lead in a film at Universal Studios, a German actor starring in an American movie, and suddenly I was "important."

Scotty, the security guard at Universal's main gate, didn't check my ID against his list of drive-on passes anymore, as he had so many times when I had guest-star jobs on the lot. Now it was a friendly smile, "Good morning, Mr. Braeden," and the gate immediately raised.

Universal Studios' top guns—Jules Stein, Lew Wasserman, and Sid Sheinberg, who'd always walked imperiously by in the commissary—invariably stopped at my booth with handshakes and cheerful greetings of "Eric! How's it going?"

Maître d's at the finest restaurants in town religiously read "the trades" and promptly led "Mr. Braeden" to their most coveted tables, with or without a reservation.

Limos were sent for studio functions and trips to the airport.

And with a few exceptions, friends began treating me a bit differently. It was subtle, but it was as if they expected me to have changed, and behaved accordingly, with a slight distance or a slight deference that had never been there before.

All in all, it was a bizarre combination of flattering, confusing, and depressing.

On one hand, there's a lot to be said for being on the receiving end of A-list treatment and a lot of attention from the movers and shakers in your industry of choice. What's not to like?

On the other hand, if you're paying any attention, there's a pervasive underlying awareness that none of it really has anything to do with you. Being declared "special" isn't a function of who you are; it's purely conditional on the size of your role in a film or television series, over which you had no control beyond your performance in a screen test. When you essentially had nothing to do with making it happen, you have nothing to do with how long it will last. It can, and often does, vanish as instantly as it appeared, on seemingly nothing more than the whim of someone you don't even know, who very likely has an agenda that would make no sense to you if you could even get to the bottom of what it is.

Then there's the odd exercise of trying to prove to your friends that you're still you, still the man you were the day before you got this job, all in an effort to erase the subtle changes you've detected between you and them and have everything get back to normal. In the meantime, new "friends" appear, some of them perfectly sincere and some of them either sycophants or predators who are sizing up your potential as a stepping-stone in their march to success. It's not always easy to tell the difference, particularly when that's not the way your mind works.

SHORTLY AFTER *COLOSSUS* CAME OUT, MY AGENT CALLED TO arrange a lunch.

It seems that producer Cubby Broccoli wanted to meet me to discuss the possibility of my being the new James Bond in the sensationally successful Ian Fleming film franchise, now that Sean Connery had decided to step aside. They were in the very early stages of preproduction on the next Bond film, *Live and Let Die,* and they needed someone to fill Connery's iconic tricked-out shoes.

It was a pleasant lunch but fairly brief.

"Do you have a British passport?" Broccoli asked.

"No," I said, "I have a German passport."

An hour after lunch ended, he called my agent to say that no one who's not a citizen of the British Commonwealth—not even an American—could play James Bond. End of discussion.

Roger Moore starred in *Live and Let Die.*

I wasn't disappointed. I'd been feeling a growing determination for quite some time to pursue projects that meant something, that were socially relevant, that *mattered,* the kind of projects that would attract the likes of Fellini or Bergman or Kurosawa.

It took me another decade or two to redefine what I've come to believe really matters in this business.

The recession of the early 1970s hit Hollywood as well as the rest of the country. I was being pursued by a small agency called Chasin Park Citron, which represented Charlton Heston, Gregory Peck, Anthony Quinn, Jimmy Stewart, and any number of other actors whose work I admired, and as soon as I signed with them, my primary agent, Herman Citron, sat me down to give me a reality check on the state of the business.

"Very few films are being made right now due to lack of money," he explained. "Some very famous, successful movie stars are going to start doing television series, which is going to compromise their careers in the long run, mark my words. You need to be patient. Films will be few and far between for a while, but they'll be back once the economy in the industry recovers. In the meantime, no television, got it?"

I listened silently, not saying a word. I understood his logic, and I respected his opinion. But none of his speculation dissuaded me from a simple, basic fact: there was no way I could promise to honor that "no television" request, not with a brand-new son to support.

6

CHRISTIAN

February 9, 1970, was and always will be the most joyful, most extraordinary day of my life, the day Christian Gudegast was born, the day I became a father.

Christian did not come into this world easily.

From the moment Dale told me she was pregnant, I couldn't wait to meet our child. I've never seen her more beautiful than she was as her pregnancy progressed, and we enthusiastically attended classes for the natural childbirth we'd set our hearts on.

We were more anxious than concerned when Dale's due date came and went, until late one afternoon, when she felt something was very wrong and I rushed her to the emergency room. While they examined her and took X-rays, I placed an urgent call to her doctor and discovered he was on vacation. I was scared, and I wasn't about to leave that hospital, or I'm sure I would have personally hunted him down and dragged him back from wherever the hell he was to help my wife.

Dale was distressed and in labor, and they admitted her into a room. I sat by her side, quietly reassuring her and using every calming massage technique I'd learned in all those natural childbirth classes, but finally, after five agonizing hours, she turned to me in panicked tears and said, "I feel he can't come out." I kept massaging her and reassuring her, but she was absolutely right—at the fifteen-hour mark, at one A.M., she'd had all she could take, and so had I.

I bolted into the hallway and told the first nurse I saw that we needed a doctor immediately. She seemed to think I was trying to start a conversation.

"What seems to be the problem?"

She was about two words into that nonsense when I shouted, "You get a doctor here *now*!"

I'd clearly frightened her, and I didn't give a damn. She ran to the nearest phone. Within minutes that felt interminable, I was watching the doctor-on-call pull Dale's X-rays out of an oversized manila envelope. His eyes widened and his face turned white, and next thing I knew he and a nurse were wheeling Dale into surgery for an emergency C-section.

I sank onto a couch in the waiting room and completely broke down.

An hour or two later I heard a voice quietly say, "Mr. Gudegast?"

I looked up to see a nurse standing there. I braced myself and held my breath.

"Would you like to come meet your baby boy?"

I'll never forget that feeling of profound, overwhelming relief. The nurse led me to the viewing room, and there lay our son, Christian, twenty-three inches long, ten pounds, blond hair, a new life, a miracle. It was indescribable to stand there gazing at him, flooded with an awareness that I would never in this lifetime experience a more extraordinary moment or a deeper connection with another human being.

Between our new baby and Dale's difficult recovery from surgery, it was both a joyful and a dramatic time, but from the very beginning we loved everything about being parents. Christian was a bright, curious, sensitive, funny child, my first thought every morning and my last thought every night. For about the first year of his life, Dale and I talked about having another baby. Then reality set in.

I was shooting a movie in Topanga with Tyne Daly when Dale began going through sharp, brutal abdominal pain. It took her doctors three or four days to figure out that her appendix was infected, apparently as a long-term consequence of her C-section. She underwent an emergency appendectomy, and once she was home from the hospital, we revisited the idea of more children. She was understandably gun-shy about going through childbirth again, and I was very worried about the possibility of her having to go through another C-section. So, without feeling shortchanged in the least, we decided that Christian would be our first and only child.

My one regret is that we didn't get to have a little girl for Dale. Here was this very feminine, very artistic woman, a brilliant cook and homemaker with no interest in sports whatsoever, devoting her life to a husband who lived and breathed sports and a son who was "all boy" from the day he was born—all without a word of complaint or even a hint of resentment. In fact, she was and is our biggest fan and most ardent supporter. She knew how many times sports had saved me, so she understood why I was so determined to make them an important part of Christian's life as well.

When the Maccabees won the National Soccer Championship in 1973, it meant the world to me that Dale and three-year-old Christian were there to share the excitement. It was probably one of the best games I ever played, from the sheer pride and exhilaration of having him there.

Christian was raised in Westwood Village—charming, *pre-developers* Westwood, truly a village back then—where we took walks on weekends with our son riding on my shoulders; where we knew all the shopkeepers and they knew us by name; and where the UCLA recreation field provided a perfect playground for me to practice soccer and for Christian to skateboard and make friends with track-and-field greats like John Smith, Russ Hodge, and Bill Toomey while they worked out. Our beautiful apartment with floor-to-ceiling windows was in a charming old Spanish building, and Mike Meyer and his wife moved in right across the street. It was an idyllic time in our lives.

I started coaching Christian's soccer team when he was five and kept right on coaching his teams until he was thirty. We made it to the final four in national tournaments twice, which was thrilling. I loved coaching him; I've just never been sure I was very good at it.

There wasn't much I didn't know about soccer, so that wasn't the problem. What completely confused me was how to be a good coach and a good father at the same time. On the way home from games, Christian would say, "How did I play?" As his coach, I wanted to be supportive. As his father, I felt I owed it to him to be honest. So I would say, "You played well, but . . ." Christian told me many years later that that "but . . ." always hung over him like a sword of Damocles.

I asked what he would have preferred, and he told me he would rather have been treated like his other teammates, something more along the lines of "Let's talk about it Tuesday at practice."

I didn't see this coming when I became a parent, but I found that line between healthy constructive criticism and discouragement to be blurry and very confusing. I still do.

I was also chagrined to discover that, as a coach, I came to a point at which I stopped hearing myself when I talked to the team. They probably stopped listening too, because I just plain ran out of original things to say. No matter how much passion you throw into delivering motivational clichés, they're still clichés. You know it, the kids know it, and yet there I'd be before a game, with the team gathered around me, ready to absorb every pearl of wisdom I had to offer, and out would come some brilliant observation like "We can do this!" or "You've worked hard, and you're ready to win!" No wonder many of them started doing impersonations of me when they thought I was out of earshot. (Actually, I have to admit, some of them were very good at it.)

It was about eight o'clock one night when Christian was in his early teens. The team was working out, and we found ourselves to be the last ones at the practice. We'd moved to the baseball diamond to practice soccer because it was the only lit area in the huge park.

We were so intent on what we were doing that we barely noticed a guy in a hoodie and jacket who came running out of the dark through the practice area, mumbling things like "You fucking dicks, you little assholes . . ." and then disappeared into the darkness.

He came close enough to us that the boys turned to each other, asking, "Did you hear that? Did he just say what I thought he said?"

I told them to just ignore him and keep playing, but before long he did it again, and again, each time getting closer and louder and more vicious with his verbal assaults on these kids. I did my best to follow my advice to the team and ignore him, but I kept thinking, "What's wrong with this idiot? Who would do that?"

And then, as he did it yet again, even closer and nastier, Christian turned toward him and said, "Please don't talk to us like that."

To which the guy loudly growled back, "I'm going to break your neck, you little fucker!" as he ran past.

That was it for me. I moved into what I knew was this guy's path, told the boys to keep playing, and planted myself there. Sure enough, here he came, out of the dark, stopped about fifty yards away from me, took off his jacket and hoodie, and started walking toward me like John Wayne. I stayed where I was, not saying a word.

He was just a few feet from me when he went into a karate stance and sneered, "What do you want, you asshole?"

He hadn't finished the word "asshole" when I hit him with a straight right, followed by a left hook and a flurry of vicious blows and kicks, and he collapsed on the ground, silent and not moving.

I immediately rounded up the team and we headed to the cars lined up on the street waiting to pick up the boys, leaving that son of a bitch right where he lay.

Later on he was picked up by an ambulance, taken to the UCLA emergency room, and kept in intensive care for a few days.

None of which I knew until a couple of weeks later, when I responded to a knock at my front door and found two cops standing there. They asked if I'd been at that specific park at about eight o'clock on the night of whatever-it-was. I said yes, I had, and invited them in.

"How the hell did you know about that?" I asked them.

They explained that the guy at the park had recognized me from *Rat Patrol* and, after being released from the hospital, had gone straight to the police.

"Of course he did," I thought, and wondered how rich that degenerate was planning to get from being punched out by an actor.

But I did what I did, and I wasn't about to deny it or, for that matter, apologize for it.

A few weeks later I got a summons from the district attorney's office to appear at a hearing in the West Los Angeles courthouse. Christian, the rest of the soccer team, their parents, and I showed up right on time. One of the fathers had called before the hearing and said, "My son told me what happened at the park that night. I want to represent you." I assured him I didn't need representation, but he was as adamant as I was. "Trust me, I'm going to be there."

So quite a crowd of boys and parents were waiting in the halls of the courthouse while the guy, the assistant district attorney, my lawyer, and I sat down at a table in a private room. The boys had already given their accounts of the confrontation at the park and what triggered it. Now it was the guy's turn.

"Well, I was running in the park, minding my own business," he told the ADA, "when suddenly these kids starting yelling at me, calling me an asshole and every other foul name in the book. And then this guy," he continued, pointing at me, "yelled, 'Come on, kids, let's get him!'"

The ADA looked as incredulous as I was. "I find that pretty hard to believe," he said. "I've actually coached soccer before, and no team I ever coached gave a second thought to someone running by during practice."

He then asked for my account of the incident, which I gladly gave in detail.

After I'd finished, my friend/attorney, who'd done his homework, turned to the guy and asked, "How many times have you been arrested, and for what?"

The guy paused, at which point the ADA reminded him that he was under oath. Finally, with audible resentment, he answered, "Three times. For assault and battery."

With that, the hearing, the guy's credibility, and any possible charges against me were over with, and the guy stormed out of the room.

As I emerged into the hallway moments later a few of the boys ran over to me and reported that as the guy blew past them he'd muttered, "You little sons of bitches, I'm going to break your necks."

I simply nodded and headed toward the courthouse exit, correctly assuming I could catch the guy as he was leaving. I stepped up to him and made him a quiet promise: "Listen carefully. One more threat, one more word out of you, and you'll be dead."

The guy walked away, and I never heard from him again.

It wasn't an idle threat. To the best of my recollection, it was the first time I realized the lengths to which I'd go to protect my son and my family. It was an extraordinary feeling, a feeling to be neither proud nor ashamed of, just a fact in the life of a father.

There was only one other time that I remember getting that angrily protective on my son's behalf, but I did a better job of suppressing it. Christian was eleven or twelve when he came home from school one day visibly upset. I asked what was wrong. He told me that a boy in his class had called him a Nazi, and he didn't understand why, or what it meant. I resisted the temptation to drive straight to that boy's house and have a meaningful talk with his parents and instead simply gave Christian the best age-appropriate explanation I could manage. He felt better, I guess, and went off to his room to do his homework, while I thought back to the long-ago afternoon when I'd asked my mother what it meant when my schoolmate confided that he was Jewish. For the first time, I related to the weariness in the sigh she gave me in response.

Among my fondest memories of Christian's childhood was taking him to my favorite boxing gym, in the ghetto at Seventy-Eighth and Hoover, starting when he was maybe seven or eight years old. It was as no-frills and unpretentious as it gets, with leaky ceilings and showers that rarely worked, a perfect respite from the slick, vapid excess of Hollywood, and it was filled with some of the warmest, most down-to-earth people I've ever met—boxer and trainer Cannonball Green; heavyweight Scrap Iron Johnson, who fought everyone from Joe Frazier to George Foreman to Sonny Liston during his career; former junior middleweight champion Eckhard Dagge, from Kiel, Germany, who became one of my favorite sparring partners; and retired lightweight Henry Davis, who trained Christian, had a Ph.D. in street wisdom, and loved to say, "Walking into the ring is like walking through fire."

When the Seventy-Eighth and Hoover gym closed down, Henry took Christian and me to another boxing gym at 108th and Broadway. Ken Norton and Michael Dokes and trainer Bill Slayton were regulars there, along with a wealth of old black fighters who would sit on the steps and play checkers, always smiling, always welcoming, always ready to tell stories and throw back their heads and laugh.

There's a stillness in a fighter's eyes when he faces an opponent, a silent calm that says, "It doesn't bother me to get hit. It doesn't bother me to get hurt." All these men knew that stillness back when they were young lions, and in sharing it, they had enormous respect for each other and for themselves. Canes, failing eyesight, slow, bent bodies and all, they held their heads high, never mourning the loss of their greatness but celebrating that they had it once, when countless others had tried and failed.

I'll always be so grateful that my son had the honor of getting to know them and experience their rare brand of dignity.

Christian and I were sparring at that gym one day when he was nineteen years old, and he absolutely nailed me with one hell of a right cross to my chin. I was still trying to shake it off when he said, "God, that felt good." I remember thinking that Freud was exactly right about the Oedipus complex, about children having an innate sense of rivalry with their same-sex parent. Christian wanted to outdo me, and I was damned glad of it. I never wanted to try to portray myself to him as some kind of superhero he could never live up to and have him spend his life chasing a ghost, a mythically infallible, unbeatable father. I wanted his love and his respect, of course, but nothing resembling awe.

Fortunately, he's also his mother's son, sharing her love of film and art and writing. When he was twelve years old, he and some friends sneaked into the back entrance of a theater in Westwood to see *The Shining*, and he announced afterward that "I'm going to make movies like that someday."

I sent him to acting school when he was in his late teens. He didn't have the slightest interest in being an actor, after living through the highs and lows of my career since he'd been born, but he agreed with my logic that it would benefit writers and directors in this business to learn all facets of their craft, including what goes into actors' performances. He studied acting, he enjoyed it, and then he followed his heart.

Christian graduated magna cum laude from UCLA, and his thesis film, *Shadow Box,* won the Best Student Film award in 1992. He sold his first screenplay, *Black Ocean,* which he cowrote with Paul Scheuring, to Oliver Stone in 1993; has gone on to sell several screenplays and to become a successful "script doctor" on major studio releases; and as I write this he's in Georgia, in preproduction on a feature film called *Den of Thieves,* on which he's both the writer and the director.

Of even more importance, he happens to be such a good man, and the person I'm closest to in this world.

And thanks to Christian and his wife, Dale finally got that little girl she so deserved, with the birth of Tatiana, the first of our three granddaughters. Those two adore each other, and I don't mind admitting that my heart melts every time that child and her sisters walk into the room.

We're a very blessed family. May there never be a day when I take that for granted.

Christian wasn't quite two years old when I was offered a role in a film called *Escape from the Planet of the Apes* in 1972. The paycheck was respectable and much appreciated, and the cast was wonderful—Roddy McDowall, Kim Hunter, Bradford Dillman, Sal Mineo, William Windom, Ricardo Montalbán, to name a few—and I liked producer Arthur Jacobs from the moment I met him.

I played Dr. Otto Hasslein, science advisor to the president, who believed that the three talking chimpanzees that arrived on Earth in an American spacecraft were a threat to the survival of the human race. Unfortunately, Dr. Hasslein was the man who shot the mother chimpanzee and her baby, so it took a while after the movie came out for me to be able to walk down the street without angry, frightened children pointing at me and yelling, "That's the guy who killed the baby chimp!"

On a few occasions I took Christian and Dale to work with me. I'll never forget watching that little boy charm the cast and crew, and stare in wonder at the "chimpanzees" who were strolling around the set between takes and stopping to talk to him. He must have thought his father's job was in some alternate universe, and it enchanted me to see the set, and the whole world, for that matter, through his wide, innocent eyes.

I grew so fond of Arthur Jacobs and his wife, Natalie, during that shoot that I actually accepted a couple of party invitations to their house.

I loathe "Hollywood parties." There's something repulsive to me about groups of overdressed people gathering to posture and drop names and blow smoke up each other's asses, trying to impress each other, lying about nonexistent screenplays they've almost finished and imaginary offers they're considering, all in an effort to get a job, or cozy up to a successful party guest they might be able to use. As far as I'm concerned, if someone wants to hire you, they'll track you down. If they don't, they won't. And sharing a plate of hors d'oeuvres with them isn't going to make a damned bit of difference.

I was prepared to politely decline Arthur's first party invitation for those very reasons, until he happened to mention that this particular party would include a Ping-Pong tournament. Really? A competition? I'm pretty good at Ping-Pong, if I do say so myself. Why, yes, come to think of it, I *am* available that night.

Before he produced the *Planet of the Apes* series, Arthur was a public relations man whose client list included Marilyn Monroe, Judy Garland, Gregory Peck, Richard Burton, Rock Hudson, James Stewart, Grace Kelly, and Marlene Dietrich. He knew everyone, and, of far more importance, he was liked, trusted, and respected by everyone he knew. So it was no surprise when Dale and I arrived at that party to find ourselves surrounded by a virtual who's who of Hollywood. No one was angling for jobs, because no one needed to. They were there out of affection for Arthur and Natalie, and it was just a fun, relaxing evening. I beat Walter Matthau and Richard Zanuck in the backyard Ping-Pong tournament but ended up losing to veteran actor Wendell Niles.

It was at a New Year's Eve party at Arthur and Natalie's house that a producer, after chatting with me for a few minutes, told me, "If you weren't German, you'd be a big star in this town." I knew he meant it as a compliment, but it stuck with me—it confirmed yet again an underlying prejudice in this industry I kept suspecting and trying to overcome.

Arthur and I had several conversations about my starring

in his next film, *Voyage of the Oceanauts,* aka *The Aquanauts.* He died of a sudden heart attack, at only fifty-one years old, before the project ever got started. It was a loss to the industry and to me personally. I'm grateful that I was given the opportunity to work with him and count him among my friends.

And come to think of it, it was a casual comment by a man at one of Arthur's parties that helped lay the groundwork for what turned out to be the role of my career.

I'll be damned.

With my father, Wilhelm, and mother, Mathilde, in Bredenbek, Germany, where I was born.

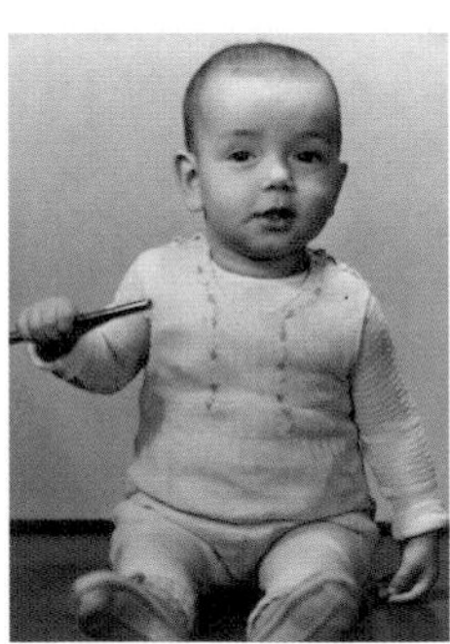

My parents named me Hans Jörg Gudegast.

This photo was taken when I was 12, shortly after my father's death. It was the most traumatic year of my life and it changed everything.

With my three brothers. (*Top to bottom:* Jochen, me, Peter, and Horst).

In 1958 I competed in the German Track & Field Team Youth Championship. I'm the fourth track team member from the right in the top row.

Throwing a shot put at the German Youth Championship in 1958.

The first fist fight in school with my childhood friend and nemesis Paul Johannsen, "Dickie" (right), and myself (left).

With my childhood friends Hildegard and Elisabeth.

Performing in the play *The Great Indoors* by Irene Kamp at the Eugene O'Neill Theater. Here I am pictured with Curt Jürgens and Clarence Williams III.

With my wife Dale at the Santa Monica Playhouse in my second play, *Kean,* by J-P Sartre, in 1963.

With onetime biggest box office star Burt Reynolds, along with all-time great NFL star Jim Brown, and Argentinian actor/funny man Fernando Lamas.

Colossus: The Forbin Project was the start of my career as "Eric Braeden." I chose "Braeden" to honor my hometown of Bredenbek, Germany.
Courtesy of Universal Studios Licensing LLC

I had the great privilege of playing Captain Dietrich, a decent, honorable German officer, in one of my first big TV credits, *The Rat Patrol.*
Left: courtesy of author. Right: © American Broadcasting Companies, Inc.

I MARRIED MY WIFE DALE IN 1966. HERE WE ARE OVER THE YEARS.

At our wedding, with Patricia Olsen (Dale's sister), my friend Michael Meyer, and Mitsu (Patricia's daughter).

OVER THE YEARS WITH MY SON AND BEST FRIEND, CHRISTIAN GUDEGAST.

TOP RIGHT: With world famous soccer player Pelé.

MIDDLE ROW (from left to right): Boxing at the Hoover Street Gym.
At Christian's wedding with Professor Michael Meyer and Restaurateur Dan Tana.

BOTTOM RIGHT: Winning The Monte Carlo Celebrity Pro Am Doubles Tournament (Left: Prince Albert of Monaco; right: Christian Gudegast).

Celebrating with my coach Max Wosniak after winning the National Soccer Championship for the Maccabees, the Jewish soccer team, in June 1973.

With tennis pro Steffi Graf at a women's celebrity tennis tournament in Toronto.

At the Chris Evert pro celeb tournament in Boca Raton, Florida, with tennis pro John McEnroe.

As Dr. Otto Hasslein in *Escape from the Planet of the Apes* in 1971.

As the character John Jacob Astor in *Titanic.* On the right, I'm standing on the Grand Staircase with Madeleine Astor (played by Charlotte Chatton).

VICTOR AND NIKKI (MELODY THOMAS SCOTT) THROUGH THE YEARS.

Top left: Tony Esparza/CBS © 2002 CBS Worldwide Inc. All Rights Reserved. Top right: Robert Voets/CBS © 2013 CBS Broadcasting Inc. All Rights Reserved. Bottom: © 2016 Robert Voets/CPT Holdings, Inc.

With former Minnesota governor Jesse Ventura.

With former president of the Soviet Union, Mikhail Gorbachev.

At the celebration of my 25th anniversary playing Victor Newman on *Y & R*. (*L to R:* gymnastics gold medalists Bart Conner and Nadia Comăneci).

© JPIStudios.com

Los Angeles City Council Member Tom LaBonge congratulating me on my 25th anniversary.

Caroline Greyshock/CBS © 2005 CBS Broadcasting Inc. All Rights Reserved.

With Chairman of the Board and Chief Executive Officer of CBS Corporation, Leslie Moonves, in October 2016 at The Paley Center for Media when CBS celebrated being #1 in Daytime TV for its 30th consecutive year.
Francis Specker/CBS © 2016 CBS Broadcasting, Inc. All Rights Reserved.

Visiting *The Talk* in February 2012.
Monty Brinton/CBS © 2012 CBS Broadcasting Inc. All Rights Reserved.

With my friend Tavis Smiley on his talk show. © *The Smiley Group/J. Van Evers*

I STARRED IN AND EXECUTIVE PRODUCED THE FEATURE *THE MAN WHO CAME BACK*.

Courtesy of author

TOP (from left to right):
With co-star Carol Alt.
With co-star Jennifer O'Dell.

MIDDLE: On the set with Larry Hinsley, Stefanos Miltsakakis, me, and Christian.

LEFT: With co-star Sean Young.

Photos in this spread by Heather Leigh Jackson unless otherwise noted.

Courtesy of author

TOP LEFT: With Oscar-winning actor George Kennedy.

MIDDLE: The cast of *The Man Who Came Back,* which was shot in west Texas.

BOTTOM (from left to right): With co-star Armand Assante.
My producing team for *The Man Who Came Back*; it was great to work with all of them as an executive producer. *L to R:* John Castellanos, producer; Stephen Bowen, executive producer and financier; me; Chuck Walker, producer and writer, and 1976 member of the U.S. Olympic Boxing Team; Sam Cable, producer.

One of my favorite photos in my collection, with my Emmy Award in the category of Outstanding Lead Actor in a Daytime Series from 1998.

Receiving a star on The Hollywood Walk of Fame in a wonderful ceremony on July 20, 2007. Arguably one of the proudest moments in my career.
© Kathy Hutchins/HUTCHINSPHOTO.com

Sean Young, Jesse Ventura, former heavyweight fighter Ken Norton, George Kennedy, and Tom LaBonge standing behind me from left to right.

With Christian at the ceremony.
Photo: sanjaynpatel.com

L to R: Professor Charles Bearchell, former German pro soccer player Dieter Hochheimer, Jürgen Jansen, me, Michael Meyer, Klaus Fredricks, former U.S. pro soccer player Albert Zerhusen, and Christian.

TOP: With my longtime publicist Charles Sherman.

LEFT: With my late *Y & R* co-star Jeanne Cooper.

Photos by Heather Leigh Jackson

THE MOST PRECIOUS GIFT A MAN CAN RECEIVE FROM HIS OWN SON.

My three beautiful granddaughters, Tatiana, Oksana, and Angelika.

7

MY TEN YEARS AS A BAD GUY

I was still looking for a project that *mattered,* but in the 1970s what mattered was supporting my family. My agent was under strict orders to let the decision to say yes or no to job offers be mine, not his. This was Herman Citron, the agent who wanted me to accept only film work because television would destroy my career. (The man was clearly not gifted at prescience.) I frankly didn't trust him not to turn down work in the name of "protecting my career" and end up "protecting" me right into the poorhouse. If an offer made sense to me, I was ready and willing to take it.

And so began a decade of guest-starring roles. Any actor

who's done a great deal of guest-star work will back me up on this: when you work on a wide variety of projects for a week or two at a time, especially if, like me, you're perpetually playing a bad guy, the vast majority of them tend to fade from your memory, often mercifully.

Some of them, though, remain memorable, for one reason or another.

Lady Ice was a film my old friend Tom Gries directed, about an insurance investigator who pursues a beautiful, wealthy young woman he believes might be fencing stolen jewels. The film itself was forgettable, but the extraordinary cast included Donald Sutherland, Jennifer O'Neill, and Robert Duvall.

We shot in south Florida, and I had the enviable task of doing love scenes with the gorgeous Jennifer O'Neill. Her fiancé was always on the set when we did those scenes, and I can't say I blamed him. Jennifer was in the stands when he and I played tennis one day. I beat him. I enjoyed that.

So yes, it was memorable to do love scenes with Jennifer O'Neill, play some tennis in south Florida, and get paid for it.

Robert Duvall and I tried unsuccessfully to get together for some tennis during that shoot, but when we were back in L.A. he invited me to his house in Bel-Air for an afternoon of doubles—me and former Wimbledon champion Alex Olmedo vs. Robert and Vincent Van Patten, a very talented tennis pro at the time who went on to beat John McEnroe a few years later and win the Seiko World Super Tennis Tournament in Tokyo. (He's now an actor, professional poker player, and poker tournament broadcaster. He met his wife, Eileen Davidson, when he appeared as her boyfriend on *The Young and the Restless.* Small world.)

Robert and Vinnie beat Alex and me that day. There was no doubt about it, Vinnie was younger and stronger than the three of us, but it was a good match and a good day.

I did five episodes of *Gunsmoke,* four of them in 1971 and the fifth in 1974. If there's an actor in this town who didn't enjoy doing *Gunsmoke,* there's something very wrong with them. The cast and crew were as welcoming and professional as any I've ever worked with, and James Arness set that tone. It seemed as if everyone involved had agreed to check their egos at the door, which made it a pleasure to arrive on the set every morning, with one exception that was completely my fault.

One of my five episodes included some scenes we shot in northern California. We spent the night at an old hotel there, and several of us found our way to the bar. By three A.M. or so, we were having ourselves a high old time, drunk and singing like a bunch of frat boys, until our producer, Leonard Katzman, later the producer of "Dallas," came across us, asked what the hell we thought we were doing, and reminded us that we were due on the set at seven A.M., wide-awake, lines learned, and ready for a long day of filming.

I slogged through the next day on three hours of sleep, with a vicious hangover. It was a long, miserable fourteen hours. I insist on believing it didn't show in my performance, but I never put myself through that self-inflicted torture again.

Northern California is beautiful, but I must admit, it was a bit upstaged by the Kahala Hilton in Hawaii, where I stayed while shooting three episodes of *Hawaii Five-O*. I certainly didn't have to be dragged to LAX. Jack Lord was all business, imperious and very precise, but for the most part the cast and crew were friendly and welcoming. I was still playing for the Maccabees at the time, and I luxuriated in doing wind sprints and working out every day on those magnificent beaches.

We'd all gather at the hotel for dinner when filming was done for the day. The restaurant was adjacent to the bar, which was always crowded with conventioneers from the continental U.S., raptly listening to a popular Hawaiian crooner who'd sing the same songs over and over again, night after night after night. I remember watching those conventioneers and thinking, "Why did you bother coming to Hawaii? You could sit in a bar and listen to a cornball singer in Omaha, for God's sake!"

I was getting somewhat spoiled by the almost vacation-like settings of location shoots, so it was a bit disappointing to learn that the episode of *Barnaby Jones*—a detective series starring Buddy Ebsen of *The Beverly Hillbillies* fame—I had signed up for was being shot right here in town, at the old Samuel Goldwyn Studios in Hollywood.

Buddy was perhaps the most laid-back actor I ever met, a very nice man who virtually sleepwalked his way through the show, with that slow, easy drawl of his.

My co–guest star was a wonderful British actor named Bernard Fox. He had a résumé as long as your arm, but he seemed to be most fondly, immediately remembered as Dr. Bombay on Elizabeth Montgomery's *Bewitched* series. He'd exaggerate his already pronounced British accent when he performed, so that even when he played a dramatic role, it could be hard to keep a straight face.

And then there was me, playing a crooked art dealer, with my clipped European accent.

So along came a scene in which I was sitting behind a desk being confronted by Buddy and Bernard about whatever it was, with a lot of grim, rapid-fire dialogue, and somehow, at the same time, the three of us suddenly became aware of how silly the combination of our accents and widely varied cadences sounded. We burst out laughing in midscene and couldn't stop. In fact, it was all we could do to even catch our breath, and as you probably know, nothing makes you laugh harder than knowing you have no business laughing.

But we were all professionals with a job to do, so finally we collected ourselves, apologized for the outburst, squared our shoulders, and started the scene again . . . only to fall completely apart even sooner this time, sides aching with hysteria, the crew laughing every bit as hard as we were.

Despite the best efforts of everyone involved, this pattern of a few lines of dialogue, interrupted by involuntary hilarity, went on for an unbelievable hour and a half. Finally the producers and a couple of executives came bursting onto the set to remind us how much this nonsense was costing, and to order us to straighten up and shoot the damned scene.

Appropriately chastened, we three grown men pulled ourselves together, took a lot of deep breaths while deliberately not looking at each other, and under the watchful, unamused eyes of the suits, launched into the scene for the thousandth time, really determined to behave ourselves and get it the hell over with.

We were rolling along quite well until, from somewhere behind the cameras, we heard a snort of laughter escape through the director's nose. Just like that, the entire sound stage burst into hysteria, including the executives, if I recall correctly.

I have no idea how we eventually limped our way through that scene from beginning to end, but I am sure that it might rank as the most time-consuming scene ever filmed on a one-hour show, and I still can't think of it without laughing all over again.

I wasn't much better at stifling compulsive laughter when I did an episode of the Darren McGavin series *Kolchak: The Night Stalker,* about a reporter in Chicago who investigates alleged supernatural occurrences. We shot that episode on the *Queen Mary,* and I played, yes, a werewolf. Hard as I tried, it was all I could do to get through my scenes with a straight face.

As a friend of mine says in response to being teased about career credits like that one, "I know why I did it. Why did you watch it?"

I thought I was doing much better at maintaining my composure on set when cameras were rolling until a few years later, when I did a film called *The Ambulance* with Eric Roberts,

James Earl Jones, and Red Buttons, and I will always maintain that this time it wasn't my fault.

The premise of *The Ambulance*, basically, was that people kept getting into an ambulance whether they wanted to or not and then disappearing. I played a doctor who was conducting some kind of preposterous medical experiment on these people, which required me to stand over their unconscious bodies holding a large syringe and then injecting them with . . . who the hell knows what?

We were all behaving fairly well in spite of the material until I had Red Buttons lying "unconscious" on a gurney in front of me. I prepared my evil syringe and was bending over to inject him when I saw his stomach vibrating with laughter under the sheet. And just like that, I was gone. He and I were in hysterics for a good five minutes before we could collect ourselves enough to get through what took maybe thirty seconds on film. Moments like that pull you right out of the scene and into the reality of what you're doing—I was no longer a malevolent doctor conducting experiments on a helpless victim. I was Eric Braeden in a lab coat, about to stick an imaginary needle into Red Buttons while he pretended to be unconscious. How much sillier can it get? But again: "I know why I did it . . ."

There was a happy coincidence on *The Ambulance*. I had lunch one day with our producer, Moctesuma Esparza. In the course of our casual conversation, I asked about his background. He was born in East L.A., he told me, and his father was a refugee of the Mexican Revolution who'd found his way to Los Angeles and worked for several years as a chef at La Scala.

To our mutual surprise, I knew his father. I worked with him at La Scala during my time as a busboy there, and I thought the world of him. In fact, Moctesuma and his father used to come to our soccer games on Sundays. Again, small world, and a valuable reminder that some very smart, very talented, very decent, hardworking people come to the United States from south of the border.

Speaking of happy coincidences, one of the nicest people I ever met was Wayne Newton, on an episode of the Robert Urich private-detective series *Vega$*. We got a kick out of discovering that we were born on the same day in the same year. I enjoyed getting to know him, and he was kind enough to invite me to his extraordinary concert in Las Vegas.

It's ironic, actually. I've always admired people who can sing and entertain like that, just as I've met several singers and entertainers who've always wanted to act.

Also on my list of "nicest people I've ever met" is Mary Tyler Moore. I did an episode of *The Mary Tyler Moore Show* and enjoyed every minute of it. I already knew and liked Ted Knight, Gavin MacLeod, Ed Asner, and Cloris Leachman, and Mary and Valerie Harper felt like old friends too, from the moment I met them. The whole group was a joy to work with.

Ed Asner and Cloris Leachman and I had actually worked together before, when we co-starred with Raúl Julía in a TV movie called *Death Scream*. It was based on the true, nationally publicized story of Catherine Genovese, a woman who was stabbed to death on a street in Queens, New York, while, allegedly, more than three dozen neighbors heard her screams and watched but did nothing to help. I came away with the greatest personal and professional respect for both Cloris and Ed, and Ed and I have enjoyed some very stimulating political discussions in the years since.

Travel was one of the perks of guest-starring roles in the 1970s, and was invariably more memorable than the projects themselves.

Mask of Sheba, for example, which I starred in with Inger Stevens immediately after finishing *Colossus,* was a TV movie shot in Acapulco. I vaguely remember that the movie was about archaeologists on an adventure or something. I remember far more clearly that Acapulco was beautiful, there were ATVs involved that were fun to ride, and because I was still with the Maccabees, I spent my downtime working out very hard and playing soccer on weekends with the residents of the slums that ran right behind the conspicuous excess of Hotel Row.

Dale, around eight months pregnant, came to visit during that shoot. The hotel doctor gave her a routine checkup while she was there. We don't know what inspired this announcement, but we've never forgotten our surprise at his simple, decisive "You have a boy."

A month later we discovered he was exactly right.

We shot a TV movie called *Honeymoon with a Stranger* in Madrid, and working in Spain has never been a chore for me.

I remember the movie being about a woman who wakes up in bed next to a man who's not her husband, but he insists he is her husband and no one will believe he's an impostor. I remember the woman was played by Janet Leigh, who brought her two little girls, Kelly and Jamie Lee Curtis.

And I remember being near the entrance of the hotel one day when a Mercedes limousine pulled to a stop at the curb. The chauffeur opened the back door of the limo and out hopped what looked like a herd of little white poodles, followed by our star, Rossano Brazzi, who was in the middle of a loud, impassioned argument, in Italian, with his wife, Lydia. She was holding her own at the top of her lungs from the back of the limo, and it was like finding myself thrust into the front row of a very noisy, very bad Italian opera.

Despite my dubious first impression of him, Rosanno turned out to be perfectly pleasant to work with and a perfectly respectable opponent during our spontaneous arm-wrestling matches on the set.

I took Dale and Christian with me to Paris, where part of the Disney movie *Herbie Goes to Monte Carlo* was shot. Don Knotts was a sweet man, Roy Kinnear was wonderful to work with, and I got to reunite with my old *Barnaby Jones* laugh-fest partner Bernard Fox.

Mostly, though, Dale and I got to experience Paris through the eyes of our five-year-old son and to introduce him, over dinner at the Café de Flore, to my cousin Rita, who of course was enchanted with him.

I met with the producers for a movie called *The Ultimate Thrill,* with Britt Ekland, whom I'd worked with on an episode of *The Six Million Dollar Man* and liked. It was shooting in Vail, which Dale and I decided would be a wonderful place to take four-year-old Christian.

"You're German, so you ski, right?" the producers asked.

I thought that was the most idiotic question, not unlike asking, "You're Swiss, so you know how to make cuckoo clocks, right?"

"Of course," I said.

I'd never skied in my life. I grew up in northern Germany, which has never been described as mountainous. My winter sport as a boy was ice hockey, on frozen ponds with makeshift hockey sticks. Skiing wasn't an option.

But since they hired me, I decided I'd better learn.

I took some lessons from an old Austrian skier named Sepp Benedikter at Holiday Hill in the mountains near Los Angeles. I was in good shape and learned fairly quickly, so Sepp suggested we take the chair lift to the top of the mountain and ski our way down.

I'd been watching that chair lift from the dining room. It looked death-defying to me. And Sepp wanted me to actually get on the damned thing after I'd only been on skis for a total of maybe one hour on the beginners hill, making pie-shaped stops? Are you kidding me? I wasn't about to let Sepp know that his suggestion had put a knot in the pit of my stomach, so I kept my mouth shut, but riding that chair lift scared the living hell out of me, and getting off of it was even worse. Skiing back down the mountain was almost a breeze by comparison. I only fell a dozen times or so, and I didn't break anything.

I must have looked a bit uneasy about the whole adventure, though, since when we walked back into the dining room, the owner asked, "First time?"

I nodded.

He shook his head and included Sepp in his pronouncement: "You guys are crazy."

That night, back in the safety of my own home and thoroughly exhausted, I called Sepp and tried to sound disappointed when I told him I couldn't make it to my lesson the next day after all.

He saw right through me. "Oh, no, you don't," he said before I even had a chance to offer the excuse I'd made up. "See you in the morning."

I went, and I survived, but I knew I hadn't quite achieved the "veteran skier" look I was hoping for, so once Dale and Christian and I arrived in Vail, I apologized to the producers for the fact that my skiing might be "a bit rusty."

I was in that godforsaken torture-device chair lift that Sunday afternoon for a practice run before filming started on Monday, and I happened to be sitting next to a woman who invited me to go powder skiing with her.

"Sure!" I said, not having the first clue what powder skiing was. At that point, what difference did it make—whatever powder skiing was, it couldn't have been any more hellish than what I'd already put myself through thanks to that ridiculous "Of course I ski!" lie.

I was wrong. Powder skiing was, as someone subsequently described it, like stirring cement. It was exhausting, it was demoralizing, and I had all that I could do to make it down that powder-covered hill without sinking waist-deep into the snow. It's an understatement to say that the thrill eluded me.

We were almost to the bottom, where several people had gathered who'd just finished their run, when I completely lost control thanks to the black diamond moguls beneath the powder, did a somersault in midair, and somehow landed on my skis.

To my shock, the crowd of onlookers burst into wild applause. I accepted it with modest "I meant to do that" grace, thinking to myself, "If you people only knew . . ."

I was still recovering from that harrowing couple of hours when I looked up the mountain to see a tiny green dot, far in the distance, zooming down the hill. Moments later I recognized it as my four-year-old son, on his little skis, in his green ski suit, flying toward me on the packed snow with the most fearless joy, having the time of his life, oblivious to the fact that skiing was supposed to be hard and that it might be dangerous.

It was an unforgettably sweet moment, a home movie I've played over and over in my mind a thousand times and always will.

Another treasured "home movie" of Christian as a child was set in Vienna, Austria, where I shot an episode of a series appropriately called *Assignment: Vienna* with Robert Conrad and Susan Strasberg.

I had some enjoyable conversations with Susan about our mutual friend Geraldine Page, and I was sorry there was no time to spar with Robert Conrad, a bona fide boxer whose television career was deservedly thriving.

We stayed at Schloss Laudon, a beautiful Romanesque hotel with a medieval gatehouse and a moat. We would go rowing on that moat at sunset when I was finished filming for the day, and I can still see Christian kneeling beside it to feed the ducks.

Lunch one day was in a picture postcard of a restaurant in the Wachau, outside of Vienna. The country setting and the Austrian white wine were unforgettable.

My agent called while we were in Vienna to tell me I was being considered for the lead role in a series. I don't even recall the name of the series, I just remember my disappointment when the part went to Robert Lansing instead, because the producer had worked with him before.

Of course, the world of prime-time television series is no more secure than any other genre in this business, as exemplified by *Caribe,* a Stacy Keach cop series that ran for only one season, in 1975, and in one episode of which I appeared. It shot in Puerto Rico, which I loved. Stacy was a very good actor and a nice man, as was series regular Carl Franklin, who went on to become a successful director as well. I had the pleasure of joining Stacy and several other actors, including Michael York and Harry Hamlin, for Sir Patrick Stewart's celebration of Shakespeare's four-hundredth birthday in 2016, and it was wonderful to reconnect with him and marvel over the fact that our careers are still going strong some forty years after we first worked together.

For the most part, my experiences in guest-starring roles in the 1960s and 1970s were perfectly pleasant. I probably did around a hundred guest spots in my career, and don't panic, I have no intention of discussing them all here. The only one that stands out as genuinely unpleasant was an episode of a series called *Matt Helm*, starring a relentlessly macho actor named Anthony Franciosa.

There was a fight scene in the script between my character and Franciosa's. I didn't think a thing about it until one of the stuntmen took me aside and warned me that Franciosa was notorious for not pulling his punches in fight scenes—he took pleasure in really punching, and punching hard.

I suggested to the stuntman that he warn Franciosa not to try that bullshit on me.

But sure enough, when the fight scene came along, Franciosa tried to hit me with a serious right cross to the chin. I managed to duck, and I pulled my punches for the first couple of takes. But by the third take, I'd had it—I left-hooked him to the liver. He folded, and while he was doubled over, I said, "Don't ever try that shit again."

He got the message.

I was pleased to discover many years later that I wasn't the only actor who felt compelled to give Anthony Franciosa a taste of his own medicine. James Garner wrote in his memoir, *The Garner Files,* that when he worked with him on a film called *A Man Could Get Killed* in the mid-1960s, Franciosa was already developing the reprehensible habit of abusing the stunt crew.

"He purposely wasn't pulling his punches during fight scenes," Garner wrote, "and he kept doing it despite my warnings to stop . . . so I had to pop him one."

I'm glad I had the opportunity to carry on the tradition.

The one job I missed out on in the 1970s that upset me was a project being developed by a producer named Skip Steloff, a series that, if I recall correctly, was going to be shot in Ireland, which I'm sure I would have enjoyed.

I don't mind losing out on a job when I'm the one responsible for losing it.

I mind very much losing out on a job when I had nothing to do with it and didn't even know a thing about it until after the fact.

One day I ran into Skip Steloff, who'd just finished producing *The Island of Dr. Moreau* with Burt Lancaster, and learned for the first time that he'd actually wanted to hire me for that series and left word for my agent to return the call to him in London.

I had a previous experience with my agent at that time, who shall remain nameless, that indicated he was shockingly cheap. I'd come straight from the set of a TV movie called *The Adulteress* with my friend Tyne Daly. I was in a hurry, on my way to visit Dale in the hospital, and I wanted to bring her flowers, which she loves. I realized I had no cash and no plastic on me and asked if I could borrow twenty dollars, which I knew he had and which he knew he'd get back. He said no. I didn't appreciate it and made a mental note of it, but I let it go at that.

Imagine my displeasure when I learned after the fact that when Skip Steloff left a message for my agent to call regarding a part for me in a series, my agent returned the call to London *collect*. It made a very bad impression on Steloff, who, among other things, couldn't imagine trying to negotiate a contract with this man, and he understandably moved on.

So did I. If I remember correctly, I changed agents within a few short hours of that conversation. The fact that that particular Steloff series never happened for one reason or another was and is beside the point.

There's no question about it, I was grateful for every acting job, paycheck, and residual check that came along. At the same time, a steady diet of guest-starring roles has its downside. It's a constant emotional roller coaster, with no guarantee at the end of any job that there's going to be another one. No matter how much logic dictates that of course there will be, you've got momentum, you're good at what you do, and word of mouth on you in the industry is all very positive, you're also aware that there's actually no logic to this business whatsoever. Even at its best, acting is a career in which financial insecurity and self-doubt are built-in occupational hazards, and guest-star roles, no matter how frequent, seem to exacerbate them.

And then there's the lack of creative stimulation, role after role that require little more than memorization, punctuality, and the ability to reliably hit your marks when the cameras are rolling. With very few exceptions, particularly doing episodic work on series television, you're there to service the plot and the series regulars, not to make full use of the skills, talent, and experience you have to offer. A point comes when it begins to feel very repetitive and very shallow, and when you're typecast as that week's villain as often as I was, you inevitably start to wonder if this is all you have to look forward to, if maybe you've already been where you're going, with no practical way to do anything about it when your first priority is always, always making sure you can provide for your family.

I thought over and over again about taking up writing, or maybe directing, anything that might reignite my fire about this business, anything that might involve me in projects that meant something and had a real impact on the audience—again, projects that *mattered*. But I kept coming up empty, and was torn between gratitude and depression. If it hadn't been for Christian, Dale, and sports, I have no idea what would have kept me going.

It was in that frame of mind that I answered a call from my latest agent one afternoon in 1980.

"They'd like to see you for a soap opera," he said.

The money aspect of it sounded mildly interesting. I agreed to a meeting, provided everyone knew right up front that whatever they had in mind, I wasn't about to commit to anything long term.

If it hadn't been for a casual conversation almost ten years earlier, I wouldn't have even known what a soap opera was.

8

MEETING VICTOR NEWMAN

It was at one of Arthur Jacobs's parties in the early 1970s that I had a casual conversation with a man who happened to be the head of daytime at NBC. He wondered if I would ever consider doing a soap opera.

"What's a soap opera?" I asked him.

He briefly explained—they were serialized stories that aired five days a week during the day, and they were quite popular.

"I've got two of them right now, *Days of Our Lives* and *Bright Promise,* and they're doing very well for us," he said. "You should stop by NBC one of these days and take a look."

I rarely pass up a chance to educate myself and satisfy my curiosity, so several days later I drove to Burbank to see what this soap-opera thing was all about. I was headed up the hallways of NBC in search of the right sound stage when a familiar voice chimed in behind me.

"What are you doing here? Slumming?"

I turned to see Dabney Coleman focusing that wry grin of his on me. Dabney and I both played tennis at the Riviera Country Club. I liked and respected him, and he was arguably the best of the celebrity tennis players at Riviera.

I explained why I was there and added, "So that's my excuse. What are *you* doing here?"

As luck would have it, Dabney was actually doing the NBC soap opera *Bright Promise.* We talked while he showed me around and told me about soaps from an actor's point of view. I honestly didn't pay that much attention, but he was encouraging about the work itself, and for me, as a new father, the steady paycheck sounded good.

"You should think about it," he told me as we said good-bye.

"I'll do that," I said, and then proceeded to get so busy, between guest-star work and my family, that I never gave soap operas another thought until that phone call from my agent in 1980 saying that someone wanted to see me about a soap called *The Young and the Restless.*

Dabney's encouragement carried a lot of weight with me, and I hadn't had the luxury of a steady paycheck since *The Rat Patrol.* So sure, why not go check it out? It wasn't as if it was going to be some long-term commitment.

I met with producers Ed Scott and John Conboy and a network executive named Nancy Wiard. After a few moments of the usual pleasantries, they had me read a couple of scenes for them and then asked if I'd mind letting them put the scenes on tape. I agreed, did the taped scenes, and left, not nervous about whether or not I'd get the job but very nervous about the idea of signing on for any length of time.

My tape was sent to Chicago for a final decision by the show's creators, a married couple named William and Lee Phillip Bell. They liked what they saw, gave me a thumbs-up, and next thing I knew, I was offered a three-month contract to appear in *The Young and the Restless* as a new character named Victor Newman.

I showed up bright and early for my first day of work, a bit shocked by the amount of memorization this job seemed to require but ready to give it a try. *Y&R* rehearsed all morning and taped all afternoon, so there would be time to work on my lines. I found some of them to be a bit awkward and stilted and revised them accordingly, and I always had preferred staying fairly loose during rehearsals and saving my actual performance for taping. I was just reviewing my scenes when a few members of that day's cast began arriving and introducing themselves:

Doug Davidson, character name Paul Williams, whom I liked immediately—he had an obvious sense of fun and loved to laugh, and he couldn't have been more welcoming;

Meg Bennett, a dark-haired beauty, smart and talented, who'd be playing my wife, Julia;

Margaret Mason, *Y&R*'s Eve Howard, Victor's secretary, a

troublemaker who'd be claiming that Victor was the biological father of her son after their one-night stand;

And then in walked a blond, smoky-voiced force of nature who studied me for a moment before walking up to me and grabbing my genitals. "Let's see what you've got, macho man," she said, and the deep, abiding friendship between me and Jeanne Cooper, aka Victor Newman and Katherine Chancellor, was off and running.

We were perhaps five minutes into my first rehearsal when executive producer John Conboy stopped me in the middle of one of Victor's speeches. His tone struck me as imperious with a touch of exasperation, as if he were straining for patience in a conversation with an idiot.

"Deliver the dialogue precisely as written, Eric."

I stared at him, looking for some sign that he was kidding. There wasn't one.

"I beg your pardon?"

"Your lines," he repeated. "Precisely as written, please. Word for word."

"I don't intend to change the intent, but as written, some of these lines are very unnatural. No one talks like that," I pointed out. He just looked at me, so I went on. "So Shakespeare often changed lines ad hoc, but that's not permitted here? Is that what you're telling me?"

"Precisely as written. Word for word," Conboy repeated, apparently having ignored everything I'd just said. "Let's proceed."

John Conboy and I were not destined to have a pleasant working relationship.

The story line that introduced Victor Newman to *The Young and the Restless* went like this:

Victor was brought to Genoa City by Katherine Chancellor (Jeanne Cooper) to help her run her company, Chancellor Industries. He and his wife, Julia (Meg Bennett), settled into the ranch he bought from Katherine and named "the Newman Ranch." Victor wanted to keep Julia all to himself out of some combination of protectiveness and possessiveness and kept her almost reclusively ensconced at the ranch while he, consumed by his new position at Chancellor Industries, was rarely there with her.

Julia happened to meet and become friends with Katherine's son Brock Reynolds (Beau Kazer), a friendship of which Victor strongly disapproved. Purely out of revenge, Victor had a one-night stand with his secretary, Eve Howard (Margaret Mason). Julia, although she was falling in love with Brock, agreed to end the friendship if Victor would recommit to their marriage. He wasn't convinced of Julia's sincerity and began pursuing local model Lorie Brooks (Jaime Lyn Bauer). Brock caught Victor and Lorie kissing and tried to reignite his romance with Julia, but in the end Julia couldn't bring herself to divorce Victor, and heartbroken, Brock left town.

In the hope of solidifying her marriage, Julia told Victor she wanted to have his baby. Victor's response was to secretly get a vasectomy.

Julia excitedly accepted a modeling offer from a good-looking photographer named Michael Scott (Nicholas Benedict). Victor didn't forbid it, and Julia proceeded to enjoy her work and become close friends with Michael.

While Victor was away on business, Eve returned to Genoa City and made it clear to Julia that she had every intention of renewing her love affair with Victor. Feeling threatened and confused by Eve's intrusion into her life, Julia had sex with Michael and was immediately overcome with guilt for cheating on her husband for the first time. Victor, back home from his trip, became suspicious of a change in Julia's tone when she talked about Michael, and he began spying on them, taping their conversations, and having them followed.

Julia announced that she was pregnant. Victor believed the baby was Michael's, kidnapped him, and held him captive in the convenient dungeon beneath the ranch house. He fed Michael just enough to keep him alive, with entrées that included a large roasted rat (bone in, medium well), kept an eye on him through the cameras he had installed in the dungeon, and took delight in torturing him with live, closed-circuit broadcasts of himself and Julia making love in their bedroom upstairs.

Julia finally discovered that Victor was holding Michael hostage, and she and Paul Williams (Doug Davidson) freed him. Victor tried to stop them, and in the struggle that ensued, Julia fell down a flight of stairs and miscarried her baby, which Victor subsequently discovered was his child, not Michael's, after all.

It's an understatement to say that after a solid decade of

playing one villain after another, I wasn't exactly enchanted with this material or with this Victor Newman character. And since soap operas were brand-new to me, I also couldn't begin to grasp the fact that from the day my first episode aired, the huge viewing audience was apparently enthralled by him—so enthralled that I was almost immediately asked to extend my contract from three months to a year.

The audience was enthralled? Really? By a philanderer who isolates his wife on a ranch, locks her alleged lover in a dungeon, and feeds him rats? What was enthralling about him, who does that kind of thing, and why was anyone buying a word of this bullshit?

As usual, it was Dale who convinced me to go ahead and sign the contract extension, by suggesting I approach these story lines I found preposterous as a challenge. "Don't be apologetic about Victor Newman," she told me, "as if you're privately winking at the audience, saying, 'I know, I don't believe this either.' Make a commitment to the material and the audience that this is who Victor Newman is and this is what he does. Period. Believe it, and make them believe it, because that's your job. That's what you've been hired to do, and obviously you're doing it right, because the audience is loving it. If you walk away after three months, you'll always wonder what you could have made of this character if you'd stuck around for a year."

I wasn't completely convinced, but I couldn't argue with her either, and a steady job and a steady paycheck for a year had their appeal.

I signed the contract extension, with reluctance.

Sometimes a seemingly negative experience can have a positive outcome.

A few months into my job on *The Young and the Restless,* I was asked to go with Doug Davidson to make a personal appearance in Toronto, Canada, at the biggest shopping mall in North America. "Personal appearance" was another new term to me, and I imagined a few rows of people on folding chairs, stopping by for an autograph on a break from their mall shopping, but with Doug along, I was confident it would at least be enjoyable.

We were picked up from our Toronto hotel and driven to a back entrance of the mall, a door wedged in among a long row of trash cans. The people who managed the complex led us into a private room, where we signed autographs for some of the mall's VIPs.

After several minutes, the local fire chief stuck his head in the door and asked Doug and me if we were ready to meet the crowds. I assumed he was being sardonic. "Sure," we said, and off we went, dutifully trailing after the fire chief down a dark hallway.

Moments later we walked through a short tunnel, with women on either side reaching out trying to grab us, and emerged into the bright light of the mall area set up for our appearance. The instant we appeared, the place exploded in a deafening cacophony of shrieks, roars, cheers, and applause that took my breath away. The throng was wall-to-wall. Even the glass elevator in the middle of the mall was packed. On the one hand, it was incredibly flattering. On the other hand, it was overwhelming, almost frightening. I didn't understand it at all.

There was no elevated stage for us—we were on the same level as the crowd. We were handed microphones and greeted everyone, then began focusing our attention on the people in the front row, most of whom were elderly, on crutches or in wheelchairs. After a few minutes of this, the back portion of the audience got impatient and began to surge forward, pushing the people ahead of them forward as well. Things quickly spun out of control, with the people in front screaming as they felt themselves being trampled from behind, and Doug and I began to literally feel as if our lives might be in danger, as if we might be crushed to death. It was one of those visceral moments I'll never forget.

I yelled at Doug, "Let's get out of here *now!*" and we escaped back through the tunnel, where the fire chief and organizers were waiting to spirit us to safety.

We were both deeply shaken and more than a little hesitant when they asked if we'd please come back for another appearance the next day. We finally agreed, on the condition that we'd be on an elevated stage and that they hire local police, football teams, or inmates to guard us. Otherwise, we'd be on the next plane back to Los Angeles.

I called Dale that night and described the chaos as best I

could. "This makes no sense to me," I told her. "All this, just for being on *The Young and the Restless*? How can that be?"

At first, as I tried to process that crowd reaction, it had a deep, profoundly negative impact on me. I'd never seen anything like it. I had spent decades being an athlete, working out and training and practicing hard in order to earn my place on two national championship teams, one in Germany in track and field and one in the United States with the Maccabees, playing before large crowds . . . and now the latter seemed pretty tame compared to those huge, wildly enthusiastic throngs I'd faced today—tame compared to that insane adulation I'd just received as a result of simply doing something I enjoyed, something that came easily to me. It seemed so illogical, so disproportionate, so unearned.

I couldn't stop thinking about it, and one indisputable fact kept intervening: by being a part of *The Young and the Restless*, I'd clearly become a part of a show people loved. For some reason or other, it was very important to them. Maybe the reason wasn't that complicated—maybe it was important to them because, for one hour a day, five days a week, it gave them stories to invest in, and characters to root for or against, and a world where they could lose themselves for a little while. Maybe it just plain entertained them, and maybe, in the end, that was enough. Maybe that's all any of us in this business should be striving to accomplish. Maybe entertaining our viewers is all that matters.

It was like a lightbulb turned on in my head. Maybe, by

joining the cast of *The Young and the Restless,* I'd finally become part of that project I'd been looking for, a project that *mattered.* I'll be damned.

That epiphany, the result of an event that struck me so negatively at first, had a very important positive impact on me and my commitment to *Y&R*. It took about twenty years for it to fully sink in, but yes, without equivocation and without apologies, we simply entertain, and that matters.

Which is undoubtedly why I have no tolerance for those in this business who view us "soap-opera people" as second-class citizens. We produce five one-hour shows a week. No one in television or film works harder than we do, and no one has a more loyal fan base with more longevity.

If anyone doubts this, come give it a try. After a few days, you'll walk away with a whole new respect for our cast, crew, and writers, I guarantee it.

Life hurtled on for Victor Newman, of course. He began building his own empire, Newman Enterprises, through any means necessary, no matter how ruthless, including the takeover of Jabot Cosmetics. Jabot was founded by Abbott family patriarch John Abbott (Jerry Douglas) as a legacy for his children, Jack (then Terry Lester), Ashley (Eileen Davidson), and Traci (Beth Maitland), and Victor's takeover was the beginning of a bitter lifelong rivalry between Victor and Jack.

In the meantime, Victor's closest friend, Colonel Douglas Austin (Michael Evans), introduced him to a young stripper at a gentleman's club called the Bayou. Her name was Nikki

Reed (Melody Thomas Scott), and Victor became enchanted with her. He launched a "Pygmalion" effort to transform her into a cultured, classy young woman, while Nikki fell deeply in love with him.

Victor and Nikki spent one passionate night together. Victor, who'd been claiming all along to have no romantic interest in Nikki, declared that night a mistake, promptly introduced her to Kevin Bancroft (Christopher Holder), and set his sights on Lorie Brooks, unaware that she was writing an exposé on him.

Nikki married Kevin Bancroft but discovered shortly after the wedding that she was pregnant with Victor's child, Victor and Nikki's daughter, Victoria.

Michael Evans, Victor's great pal Colonel Austin, was a delight, a great foil for Victor and a true professional whose lengthy résumé included *Gigi* on Broadway with Audrey Hepburn. He had a quick, dry British wit, and I loved working with him. I was very sad when he passed away in 2007.

For the most part, I had the greatest respect for my coworkers. (My relationship with John Conboy continued to suffer from a failure to thrive.) The work was very demanding, and I've never backed off from demanding work. The steady salary was affording my family a nice, secure lifestyle, with the added bonus of a healthy college fund for Christian. But by the time that first year on *The Young and the Restless* drew to a close and I was being asked to sign a new long-term contract, I was having serious doubts about my interest in sticking around.

I'd begun to sink into a depression, not over the work itself but over what I perceived to be the lack of depth in the Victor Newman character. More and more, I felt I was playing a dehumanized man who could be cold, cruel, manipulative, and amorally shrewd, for no other reason than because he could. I didn't understand what on earth was driving this man, or, as an actor, what range there was to play in Victor Newman beyond his two most prominent qualities: charm, and a megalomaniacal need for control. If that's all he was and all he was ever going to be, there wasn't enough substance there to inspire me to continue, let alone on a long-term basis.

Bill Bell, the show's brilliant creator and head writer, flew to Los Angeles from Chicago to meet with me, and I explained my reluctance to stay on *The Young and the Restless.*

"What do you need?" he asked. "What can I do?"

"You can make Victor Newman a whole person," I told him. "You can give him a backstory, a history that will let me and the audience understand what motivates this man, what keeps him from being just another TV villain no one including me can possibly invest in or care about in the long run."

He got it immediately. "I'll do it," he said.

He was a man of his word. He did it, and did it beautifully.

Victor's backstory was revealed in a scene between him and Nikki Reed (Melody Thomas Scott), the woman who would go on to become the great love of his life. They were spending their first Christmas Eve together, and Nikki, sensing a deep pain beneath Victor's seemingly impenetrable surface, urged him to tell her about his past.

Finally, with great reluctance and tears in his eyes, Victor opened up to her.

He was born Christian Miller, he told her, the son of Albert and Cora Miller. Albert was a drunk who deserted his wife and left her destitute. Unable to provide for her son, Cora left him in an orphanage when he was seven years old. He grew up determined to be "victorious" over his upbringing, an unbeatable success to whom family would mean everything, not a grown-up version of a lonely, abandoned child but a "new man." When he was old enough to leave the orphanage and strike out on his own, he renamed himself "Victor Newman," fiercely protective of what was his, and fearless, sure that there was nothing worse life could do to him that he hadn't already survived.

I loved it. Victor Newman was now a multifaceted man with authentic motivations and many levels to play, and I felt a whole new excitement about him. I also related to him personally, of course, from my being so young when my own father died and knowing the pain of feeling abandoned and of living impoverished.

I still remember going to my dressing room after that Christmas Eve scene and knowing, beyond any doubt, that I was going to stay on *Y&R* and explore that character. And then along came the other deciding factor in my decision to stay: John Conboy left *The Young and the Restless* to executive produce a new soap opera called *Capitol,* and a very talented, personable man named Wes Kenney came in to take his place. Wes was an absolute pleasure to work with, open to collaboration and to anything and everything that was in the best interest of the show. He listened to input from the cast and gave us honest feedback—if we made a suggestion that wouldn't work, he'd say so and explain why rather than simply rejecting it out of hand. If our suggestions, including changes in dialogue, improved the show, he'd gladly approve them. He made a world of difference in my enjoyment of going to work, and we were lucky to have him.

The Victor Newman backstory led to a couple of the most memorable acting experiences of my career.

Not long after Victor and Nikki's wedding (the first of many), Nikki, with the help of private investigator Paul Williams (Doug Davidson), arranged a reunion between Victor and Cora Miller, the mother he hadn't seen since she left him at the orphanage when he was just seven years old.

The reunion started out as a disaster. Victor, who was a self-made billionaire by then, assumed this woman was just another con artist with just another scheme to get her hands on his money. He was dismissive of her until she mentioned a hole in a sweater, something only his mother could possibly have known, and he realized it was really her, it was really the woman who'd given birth to him and then abandoned him. Then his pain rose to the surface, in the form of rage, and he told her he never wanted to see her again for what she'd done to him as a young, helpless child.

It was as powerful a sequence as I've ever performed, emotionally satisfying and beautifully written, full of hurt and anger and sadness and a lifelong yearning for a mother's love, and it deeply touched me. When I first read it I had no idea how I was going to play it, and beyond learning the lines, I didn't prepare for it. I just know that when we shot it, I was completely immersed in it. I felt every bit of every moment from the inside out.

Victor subsequently learned that Cora was dying of cancer and brought her to the ranch, where she met her granddaughter, Victoria, and spent her final days. Dorothy McGuire was wonderful, and I'll never forget the whole rich experience of working with her.

Another series of memorable scenes that came from the backstory Bill Bell created were shot in 2003, when Victor flew with his son, Nicholas, to Canada to meet Victor's father, Albert Miller, the man who abandoned his wife and children all those years ago and went on to become a very wealthy man without a single glance back at the family he left behind. Victor's father was played by none other than the late, great George Kennedy.

I had such admiration for George Kennedy. He was obviously an incredibly accomplished actor, with a career that spanned almost six decades and included such acclaimed series as *Dallas* and *The Blue Knight* and an Academy Award for his role in *Cool Hand Luke* with Paul Newman. He was also an utter gentleman, with a heart as big as he was, and a real pro—he was a newcomer to the toughest medium in television and film, and he arrived on set fully prepared, numerous lines learned and performed to perfection.

Albert Miller was one cold, remorseless son of a bitch, a man Victor couldn't begin to comprehend, let alone forgive, and they were raw, tragic scenes to play, the kind of scenes that occasionally remind me what a pleasure it is to be an actor.

ALBERT: What do you want from me now, Christian Miller? Money? I'm a wealthy man. A million dollars. Two million. Name your price. I'll write you a check and then you can go.

VICTOR: I want nothing from you. I'm no longer Christian Miller. I'm Victor Newman. I'm *the* Victor Newman. Do you understand that? I've made my own life. I'm wealthy beyond your wildest dreams, and respected, and known around the world. Perhaps I should thank you for the pain you have caused me, for the cruelty you have done to me, because without that I would not be the man I am now. And without the pain I have carried with me all my life, I would never have realized that none of it means anything, no wealth means anything without family. I came to say good-bye to you, and I've said my good-bye.

ALBERT: Don't come back. Do you hear me?

VICTOR: Why would I ever come back to see you?

My tears at the end of those scenes were as real and heartfelt as any I've ever experienced as an actor.

George and I became friends after working together on *The Young and the Restless.* I had the good fortune to work with him again years later, on my film *The Man Who Came Back.* His passing in 2016 was both a professional and a personal loss to me.

Rest in peace, my friend.

9

"I'M GOING TO MAKE YOU PROUD"

In 1986, during my sixth year on *The Young and the Restless,* my mother passed away at the age of seventy-eight.

It hit me hard.

She was living alone in Bredenbek, in the house I bought for her. She'd spent much of her adult life yearning for her sons to come visit her. While I will always love my hometown and its people, I grew up knowing I wouldn't be staying there, that I would never be content if I didn't satisfy my curiosity and drive to experience all those distant places beyond the horizon, but it was still sad for me to see her so infrequently. She died having met my wife and son, and I find peace in that.

She clearly knew death was coming. She'd written out instructions for her funeral that were so specific, so organized, and so like her that it made my brothers and me smile, everything from what the pastor should say about her from the pulpit to how many cognacs each mourner was allowed at the local inn after the service—those who lived close by could have two, while those who lived farther away were permitted only one.

It was deeply moving to see so many old, familiar faces I'd known all my life, neighbors and farmers from far and wide, gathered in my childhood church and at the gravesite beside my father's to pay their final respects to her. It took me back to the countless times I'd gone riding through the countryside on my bicycle as a boy, always ending up at my father's grave in an effort to feel close to him and fill the emptiness in me that his devastating death left behind. It's a ritual I've continued on every trip home to Germany, still making the same promise I made to him at the age of twelve: "I'm going to make you proud."

My father didn't live long enough to see me excel at sports. In fact, like most German families throughout my school years, mine was absent at all my athletic events, with one exception—my mother did show up once, for about twenty minutes, at a regional track meet and saw me compete in discus, javelin, and shot put. Other than that, one of the many things I appreciate about America is the enthusiasm parents feel and the involvement they show in their children's sports activities, and it's one of the reasons I made such a point of being involved in Christian's athletic pursuits. It's a lonely feeling to be competing on the field and doing your damnedest to win, only to glance over and see not one family member in the stands, and I never wanted him to experience that.

I suppose there's a certain symmetry in the fact that *The Young and the Restless* never aired in Germany, so my mother never saw a single episode, but she did take pleasure in knowing I'd become a success at my chosen career.

One day not long after I returned from my mother's funeral, I was driving from Los Angeles to Palm Springs on my way to a celebrity tennis tournament, looking forward to playing with some of the usual suspects like my old pal Dabney Coleman, John Forsythe, Elke Sommer, Doug McClure, and Charlton Heston. It was a spectacular day. The sky was a bright clear blue, and recent rain had created a lush green landscape. I wasn't consciously thinking of my parents, but suddenly, out of nowhere, I almost tangibly felt their presence, more strongly than I'd ever felt it before. They were together, smiling down at me with the purest, most unconditional love, and it filled me with a surge of renewed motivation I'll never forget. "I'm going to make you proud," I promised again, this time to both of them, the two people who gave me life.

As my humanitarian activism reignited in the late 1980s, I thought of that promise countless times, determined to keep it.

In September of 1987, I was interviewed by a man named Michael E. Hill for an article in the *Washington Post*. I've never been shy about expressing my opinions when talking to the press, and that interview was no exception. The ostensible subject of the article was the popularity of Victor Newman on *The Young and the Restless,* but it evolved into a conversation about my chagrin at the clichéd image of Germans in America, the idiotic, offensive assumption that "German" and "Nazi" are synonymous, and about my awareness that while it was infuriating, it was also understandable.

"After all is said and done," I told him about the Hitler regime, "what you can't escape is the extent and degree of its viciousness and racist attitude. There's no getting around the fact that it happened. If there's anything to the saying that the sins of the father are visited on the son, this is such a case, and I have to live with that."

The day that issue of the *Washington Post* was published, I got a call from a man named Günther van Well, the former German secretary of state who was now the West German ambassador to the United States. He'd read the article and was very complimentary about my willingness to discuss the vilification of Germans while so many were reluctant to even acknowledge it, let alone to the press.

He invited Dale and me to a dinner party at his home in Washington, D.C., and we happily accepted. It was an exciting, stimulating evening, with a guest list that included Senator William Fulbright of Arkansas, who, in addition to being the former chairman of the Senate Foreign Relations Committee, created the international student-exchange program called the Fulbright Scholarship. I had some fascinating conversations with the other guests about the dangers of oversimplifying history and judging anyone based on narrow-minded, uneducated generalizations. "I'll be damned," I told them, "if I'm going to tolerate my image being defined by the Nazis." It was a pleasure to spend a few hours in the company of a group of erudite people who weren't interested in just talking about issues; they were interested in actively addressing them and finding ways to deal with them.

Dale and I returned to Los Angeles and I went back to work on *The Young and the Restless* with pleasant memories of that dinner party, expecting nothing more to come of it. So it came as a very flattering surprise when the subsequent German ambassador, Jürgen Ruhfus, and his wife, Karin, invited Dale and me to a gala in Washington. Ruhfus was a lawyer, the former ambassador to London and Paris, and a foreign policy and security advisor to German chancellor Helmut Schmidt, as welcoming as he was accomplished. He and I met several times after that first evening, getting acquainted and exchanging ideas, and in 1987 he honored me with an appointment to the German American Advisory Board; among my fellow board members were General Alexander Haig, secretary of state under President Ronald Reagan; Katherine Graham, publisher of the *Washington Post;* Dr. Henry Kissinger, secretary of state under Presidents Richard Nixon and Gerald Ford, national security advisor, and Nobel Peace Prize winner; number one tennis great Steffi Graf; and Paul Volcker, chairman of the Federal Reserve.

The German American Advisory Board met several times at Blair House in Washington, D.C., with West German president Richard von Weizsäcker, who in my opinion symbolized the best of German society after World War II. He'd actually fought in that war and was an extremely bright, thoughtful, thought-provoking man.

I expressed to him on more than one occasion how much I wished he would make himself available to American talk shows. With just a few appearances he could have helped dispel for millions of people the ugly, stereotypical image of Germans as just a stern bunch of goose-stepping Nazis. He was a popular speaker at Harvard, Princeton, and other American universities, but limiting his speeches to halls of academia, essentially, as they say, preaching to the choir, barely scratched the surface of his potential impact in this country.

Much of the reason for his lack of exposure on talk shows and popular media, as far as I was concerned, was the weakness of the bureaucratic German Information Service. "Mr. President, if you want to improve Germany's image in America, you need to fire those bureaucrats and hire a successful U.S. public relations firm," I told him. "I promise you, when the German Information Service calls the *New York Times* or the *L.A. Times* or a producer at the *Tonight Show* and announces, with a thick German accent, 'Our president, or our ambassador, or whoever is going to be in your city next week,' the person who takes the call will be perfectly pleasant on the phone. Then they hang up and tell their coworkers, 'Another fucking Nazi is coming to town.'"

I believed then and I believe now that the image of Germans could have been humanized much more quickly by familiarizing the American public with some of the impressive, accessible German leaders of the past several decades, and the right American PR firm could be a huge step toward making that happen.

President von Weizsäcker didn't disagree, but he regretfully added that it would be very difficult to persuade the bureaucratic German parliament to remove the bureaucrats from the German Information Service—not a verbatim quote, simply my interpretation of his response.

My conversations with him were emotionally and intellectually inspiring, as were my many interactions with the German American Advisory Board, and one of the most enthralling evenings of my life, a result of my involvement with the Board, was a gala at the Kennedy Center. Dale and I mingled with a veritable who's who of Washington, D.C., followed by enormously conciliatory speeches from President von Weizsäcker, Dr. Kissinger, and others, culminating in a spectacular performance by the Berlin Philharmonic of Beethoven's unifying Ninth Symphony, which moved all of us to tears in that great hall.

The next morning I eagerly read both the *New York Times*

and the *Washington Post* from cover to cover, expecting to find rave reviews of that extraordinary evening. But other than a few lines about the performance of Beethoven's Ninth, there was nothing—not a word about the event, its purpose, those wonderful speeches, nothing. Typical, I thought. Par for the course.

That afternoon I was interviewed by Larry King on his radio talk show. He led off with the question "What brings you to Washington, D.C.?" I told him about the Kennedy Center event, to which he replied, "I didn't know anything about it."

"I'm not surprised," I told him. "It was a positive evening about Germany, so no one was interested in talking about it."

And off we went into a fascinating hour of discussion about German/American/Jewish relations, which Larry later described as one of the most interesting interviews he'd ever done.

Similarly, a wonderful, star-studded reception was held one night at Los Angeles' Getty Center for German chancellor Angela Merkel, a truly remarkable woman.

The following day the *Los Angeles Times* covered this distinguished event . . . in a four-line article. *Four lines,* to report about the local presence of one of the most important leaders of the Western world. Presumably the *Times* needed the space for a more pressing story like some reality star changing her hair color.

Whatever the case, in my opinion it was just another typical display of laziness, ineptitude, or both, on the part of the German Information Center.

Not long after the Larry King interview, Ambassador Ruhfus asked if I would be interested in creating a German American Cultural Society. I said yes, but insisted its purpose be to promote and encourage open-minded German/American/Jewish dialogue. The proposition intrigued me enormously. I discussed it with my friend Mike Meyer, who was as intrigued as I was, and it was gratifying to discover that a lot of Germans, German Jews, and Americans from many walks of life, including professors Cornelius Schnauber of USC, Hans Wagner of UCLA, Jeanette Arens, Jürgen Janson, Wolfgang von Chmielewski, Alexander von Wechmar, and other members of the intellectual community, were interested as well. By then Dale and Christian and I had moved to a wonderful, refreshingly private house in Pacific Palisades, and the German American Cultural Society was officially convened in our backyard and continued for many, many years.

On November 9, 1989, some very positive headlines about Germany captured the world's attention. Brokered in large part by President Ronald Reagan and General Secretary of the Soviet Union Mikhail Gorbachev, and signaling a thawing of the Cold War across Eastern Europe, the checkpoints across the Berlin Wall were thrown open. Celebratory East and West Berliners flooded through those checkpoints, and the reunification of Germany was officially under way.

While I was deeply proud of and committed to the German American Cultural Society, I've never been content to limit my strongly held beliefs to conversations in backyards full of like-minded friends. Reenergized by all the doors that had been thrown open to me as a result of that *Washington Post* interview, and by "the Fall of the Wall," I began accepting invitations to deliver a speech I wrote called "Thoughts on Being German."* It spilled out of me in one sitting in a San Francisco hotel room the night before my first speaking engagement. It was a reflection on my own personal experiences and, as a result, seemed very specific, but its intention was a much broader commentary on the cruelty and potential tragedy of collective condemnation, making snap assumptions about people based on superficial labels without investing the time, energy, and sensitivity to discover who's really "in there."

My heartfelt efforts, motivated by nothing more and nothing less than my passion for promoting a positive, realistic image of Germans in America and advancing German/Jewish dialogue, resulted in my being awarded the Federal Medal of Honor by the president of Germany.

As I walked to the podium to accept that award, I'm sure a part of my heart was aware of the boy in me, determined to keep a promise to his parents to make them proud, and of the actor in me, well aware that the spotlight on me, starting with that *Washington Post* article, was there because I was chosen by Bill Bell to share it with a character named Victor Newman on *The Young and the Restless.*

Even on my worst days at the studio—and yes, I have my share of them—I am and will always be very, very grateful.

---

* *The speech in its entirety can be found in Appendix A.*

10

"VICTOR! VICTOR! VICTOR!"

While all that was going on, Victor Newman, in his way, was as busy as I was.

After surviving an attempted poisoning and being shot with a harpoon while rescuing Nikki from a scorned lover who was holding her hostage on St. Croix, Victor married Nikki in a beautiful ceremony at the Colonnade Room, back in the days when *Y&R* still spent money on that kind of thing. He'd reunited with his mother and his younger brother Matt Miller (Robert Parucha) by then, and he put Matt in charge of one of his Brazilian companies.

In the meantime, Ashley Abbott was stricken with amnesia and subsequently kidnapped. Ashley's (ostensible) father, John, contacted Victor, who found her and brought her back to the Newman Ranch to recuperate from the trauma. She left the ranch when she realized that she and Victor were starting to fall in love. Nikki had already figured this out and, seeking revenge, had an affair with Ashley's brother Jack. Then she changed her mind and realized she wanted Victor after all, and she tried to promote a romance between Ashley and Victor's brother Matt. But there was no stopping Victor and Ashley—they were in love, and Victor and Nikki separated.

Then Victor learned that Nikki had cancer, and he went back to her, still loving her and wanting her to spend her final days on earth knowing that.

Ashley didn't learn about Victor and Nikki's reconciliation until after she discovered she was pregnant. Matt offered to marry her, but she decided she had no choice but to abort Victor's baby.

Nikki went into remission but failed to tell Victor, believing that if he knew her health was no longer in jeopardy, he might leave her and go back to Ashley. He found out she was now faking her disease, and Nikki's greatest fear became a reality—he filed for divorce and planned to reconcile with Ashley. But on finding out that Ashley aborted their baby, he flew into a rage, which traumatized her into amnesia again and she ended up in a mental institution.

Victor's archenemy, Ashley's brother Jack Abbott, hired Leanna Randolph to write a tell-all biography called *Ruthless: The Victor Newman Story,* under a pseudonym. Through an uncanny coincidence, Victor hired the same woman to write his authorized biography. Leanna, behind Jack's back, added an extra chapter to *Ruthless* exposing Ashley's affair with Victor as well as the resulting abortion.

Nikki was pregnant again, with Victor's baby, and she had her heart set on reconciling with him. But when *Ruthless* came out, Victor wrongly concluded that Nikki was responsible for it, immediately proceeded with their divorce, and to everyone's surprise, married Leanna.

Leanna had fallen in love with Victor and felt so guilty about the vicious book she'd written about him that she wrote another one under her own name, called *Victor Newman—Man and Myth*.

Victor, to take revenge on Jack for being the brains behind *Ruthless,* cleverly manipulated a takeover of the Abbott family company, Jabot, demoted Jack, and hired Brad Carlton (Don Diamont) as Jack's new boss.

Victor and Nikki's baby was born while they were apart, a son named Nicholas Christian Newman (eventually Joshua Morrow).

Jack found out that Victor was planning to ask Nikki to marry him again and quickly married her himself. Victor had a contract drawn up in which he promised to return Jabot to the Abbott family if Jack would divorce Nikki.

Jack was in love with Nikki, but he was also willing to sacrifice his own happiness if it meant getting back the company his father founded and worked so hard to build as a family legacy. Jack signed the contract, not noticing a shrewdly worded clause that made it null and void.

Nikki became pregnant by Jack but miscarried after a fall from a horse, and as a result she became addicted to pain pills and alcohol. Victor tried to rescue her from her addictions, at the same time discovering that Jack and Brad were plotting a takeover of Newman Enterprises. Victor and Jack had a fierce argument that caused Victor to collapse, and Jack simply stepped over him and walked out, leaving him there to die. Ultimately, Jack's conscience demanded that he summon help after all, and Victor was saved.

Jack finally left Nikki when it became clear that her heart would never really belong to anyone but Victor. But Nikki, Ashley, and Victoria (Heather Tom) were all furious with Victor for the variety of ways in which he was trying to control their lives, and he left town angry and disgusted.

He eventually found his way to a farm in Kansas, where he met and fell in love with Hope Adams (Signy Coleman), his future wife and the mother of his son Adam, while everyone in Genoa City believed that Victor Newman was dead.

If you think I put all that together from memory, you're giving me more credit than I deserve. But it's interesting to look back on where Victor Newman has been and, as a result, the stories I've been given to play as an actor, and the stories that attracted such loyal, enthusiastic audience response from such a wide variety of people.

The myth that soap operas are watched exclusively by bored housewives and nursing-home residents is as infuriating as it is pure fiction, and I have no patience with it. It's insulting to those of us who work in the soap industry, and to our viewers, to even imply that *Y&R* owes its popularity to people who have no lives.

I still remember driving along in Hollywood one day when a chauffeur-driven Rolls-Royce with tinted windows maneuvered through traffic to pull up beside me. The occupant in the backseat rolled down the window and there was "The Hitman" himself, Tommy Hearns, the first boxer in history to win world titles in five weight divisions. He yelled out, "Victor! My man! Anytime you start having trouble with all those women, give me a call!"

Ron Harper of the Chicago Bulls walked up to me on the street one day and introduced himself, and then called his mother to brag that he'd just met Victor Newman.

I'd heard that former professional wrestler, Vietnam veteran, and governor of Minnesota Jesse Ventura was a fan of the show. I had my publicist contact him, with the ultimate result that he appeared on *The Young and the Restless,* playing himself, suggesting that he and Victor run together in the upcoming election. I found Jesse to be an honest, independent man who speaks his mind; we became friends and it was my pleasure to fly to Minnesota to attend his fiftieth birthday party at the governor's mansion.

I was told that St. Louis Cardinals Hall of Fame pitcher Bob Gibson called home when the team was on the road to find out if Victor had left Hope yet.

Two-time world heavyweight champion and Olympic gold medalist George Foreman surprised me at the studio one day. He was shown into my dressing room, introduced himself, shook my hand, and said, "I'm honored." I was blown away and replied, "Are you kidding? *I'm* honored."

Sports Illustrated ended up doing an article about the popularity of Victor Newman and *The Young and the Restless* among athletes in practically every sport imaginable, and I must say, it was very gratifying to be recognized by men I recognized and respected.

Stars in the music industry have been among *Y&R*'s most loyal fans, from the incomparable Aretha Franklin to James Brown and Little Richard, both of whom visited the set. I had the great pleasure of being introduced to another of the show's fans, B.B. King, in Memphis. Physicians, teachers, factory workers, corporate executives—there really is no such thing as a "typical" fan of *The Young and the Restless*. When the personal appearances I do are not too chaotic and the lines aren't too long, I still enjoy asking people what they do for a living, and the variety of answers never ceases to fascinate me.

Bill and Lee Bell understood that when they created *Y&R*. Bill understood it when he wrote the show. He never wrote "down" to his audience. He wrote with respect for their intelligence, and for the innate, complicated integrity of his core characters. Some of our subsequent writers have carried on that tradition. Some haven't. And rest assured, a few of us core characters have been as vocal as the fans when it comes to protecting the Bells' creation and our decades-old investment, for all the good it sometimes does.

I knew that *Y&R* was enjoying widespread international popularity in the 1990s, but it still came as a very pleasant surprise to learn one day that we had a special visitor to the set—the sister of Israeli prime minister Shimon Peres, a woman who made no effort to disguise her excitement at meeting Victor and Nikki and Katherine Chancellor and Paul Williams and the Abbott family. It was charming and very flattering, and it ultimately led to a conversation between me and Israeli diplomat Yuval Rotem, a wonderful man, about the possibility of my visiting Israel. I assured him that I'd be delighted, and we began making arrangements.

Before I left for Israel, I was interviewed by a columnist for a newspaper in Tel Aviv. A few weeks later the columnist called back, embarrassed and apologetic. It seems the paper's headline editor had added his own twist to the article. "I'm so sorry," the columnist told me, "but the headline says that Eric Braeden's father was a Nazi." He was eager for me to know that he had nothing to do with the headline, he apologized again, and he hoped I wouldn't cancel my trip but would understand if I did.

I assured him that I was used to this sort of thing and added, "Not only am I not canceling my trip, but I'm definitely coming now, if you'll kindly arrange a press conference for me when I get there."

He did exactly that, and I was promptly escorted to a press conference when I arrived in Tel Aviv. I addressed the headline and then asked rhetorically, "Is it really in Israel's best interest to perpetuate this image of all Germans being Nazis . . . any more than it's helpful when others perpetuate Jewish stereotypes? What possible good does it do? Isn't it time we stop this?"

I repeated those sentiments after visiting Yad Vashem, the Holocaust museum in Jerusalem. There aren't words to describe the shattering impact of all those artifacts from one of the most obscene, tragic, soul-wrenching eras in human history, so it was difficult to express it to the press when they asked what I thought of it.

I told them that obviously I was deeply affected, just as I'd been when I went to the Holocaust museum in Washington, D.C. How could anyone of the German postwar generation not be deeply affected, and filled with some combination of sorrow and rage, by what was done in the supposed name of the German people?

One thing that bothered me in the Jerusalem museum, though, I told the press, was that the comments throughout the tour referred to "Germans," when I felt it was incumbent upon them to be accurate and use the word "Nazis" instead.

"You must remind people of the fact that Jews were probably more successfully assimilated into German society than anywhere else in the world," I said. "That's an historical fact. What that Austrian son of a bitch did in Germany in a twelve-year period is still beyond comprehension, and it's hardly an objective, accurate picture of what Germans felt about Jews prior to World War II. Please let your museum be specific about that and point to the people who were actually culpable—Nazis, not Germans.

Germany has been supportive of Israel on so many levels after that war. If you don't acknowledge it, you're likely to evoke a reaction from Germans that 'whatever we do isn't good enough, so why bother?' That's in neither your best interest nor ours."

The director of the museum very graciously shook my hand, thanked me, and best of all, agreed with me.

It may not have been the most politically correct moment of my life, but in the shadow of a building filled with artifacts from the most unspeakable horror ever committed against humankind, it seemed even more important than usual not to tread lightly, not to weigh each and every word with such caution that I'd end up saying absolutely nothing of any significance. I believe in open and honest discourse. I believe in having the courage to say what we mean and mean what we say, and giving other people the opportunity to do the same. Ultimately, I believe that underneath it all, underneath a lot of cultivated superficial assumptions based on nothing meaningful whatsoever, most of us have a great deal in common. Discovering what that is, is the quickest way I know to put a stop to the dehumanization that leads to bigotry, racism, and the blind, ignorant sense of superiority that once upon a time metamorphosed into the Holocaust. May it never, ever happen again.

I never have and never will try to whitewash Germany. Yes, there is anti-Semitism there, and the fact that it's less prevalent than in other countries doesn't excuse it. Yes, there were Germans who were complicit with the Nazis. Many of them were good, decent people like my father, who didn't have an anti-

Semitic or violent bone in his body and simply bought into Hitler's propaganda-driven economic, anti-Communist agenda without a clue about the nightmare that madman was planning to unleash. And I'm sure there were Germans who were anti-Semitic but would have been horrified by the annihilation of Jews, while others quite willingly, and tragically, participated in the Holocaust. There are gradations when it comes to any prejudice—not every anti-Semite in Germany was a despicable war criminal, just as not everyone who's prejudiced against blacks, let's say, has a cross burning in their front yard.

Sadly, I don't know of any nation or any society that's completely prejudice-free. I even had a teammate on the Maccabees who was an Ashkenazi Jew and prejudiced against Sephardic Jews—oh, and Ethiopians as well, come to think of it. It just goes on and on, and I'm afraid it always will until, again, we stop falling into the shallow, ignorant trap of collective condemnation, start meaningfully communicating with each other to get beyond what we are and learning *who* we are, and above all, stop expecting so little of ourselves that we'll tolerate even a moment of racism, in ourselves or in anyone else.

In my opinion, one of the most impressive men in the second half of the twentieth century was Israeli's prime minister at the time, Shimon Peres, so it was with the greatest pleasure that I accepted an invitation to meet with him in his office.

He was a mensch, wise and noble and articulate, a genuine human being with an accessible soul, the antithesis of the bureaucratic cartoons we've all suffered through who are so in love with the sound of their own voices that they believe they're the most qualified leaders simply because they're the ones who make the most noise.

Prime Minister Peres and I sat and talked for quite some time, and I'll never forget an extraordinary moment that occurred. As we conversed, I pointed out that I was born in a country that was responsible for the most cataclysmic war the world has ever seen, but that country was now partners with its archenemies, England and France, in the European Union.

"Forgive me my question, Mr. President, but don't you think it might be possible in Israel to initiate a Middle Eastern common market of great mutual interest? Historically, this is one of the most extraordinary areas of the world. If there were peace in the Middle East, imagine the potential just for the tourism industry alone, which would be of enormous benefit to everyone."

He sat silently for a thoughtful moment, then walked to the window and gestured for me to join him there. He pointed down to a specific place on the street below.

"That is the spot where my friend Yitzhak Rabin was killed."

That's all he said.

That's all he needed to say.

Yitzhak Rabin was assassinated by an Israeli extremist who was radically opposed to Rabin's peace initiative between Israel and Palestine.

Jerusalem is a beautiful city, and it breaks one's heart that it's divided by walls. It's hard to describe the overwhelming awareness that overcame me, a kind of awe at being in a place of such extraordinary historical significance to the world's greatest religions. I found myself with tears in my eyes more than once, thinking of all the violent wars that have been fought in the name of religion. How is it not a tragic oxymoron to even use the words "war" and "God" in the same sentence, or "war" and "Jesus," whose message was love and forgiveness, not rage and bloodshed? And why, in the wake of those wars, do people ask, "How could God let this happen?" as if God had anything to do with it? Maybe as long as there are human beings, there will be conflict, but what a shame for us to expect so little of ourselves and not hold ourselves to a higher standard.

From the Wailing Wall to the Dome of the Rock to the poignant sound of the daily call to prayer by the Muslims, there's a longing, a sense of eternity, throughout Jerusalem that's intensely stirring. I was lost in that almost disquieting feeling of connection to something beyond our comprehension one day when I was walking along the Via Dolorosa, historically the path that Jesus walked, bearing the cross, on his way to his crucifixion. But I was shocked back to the present when shop owners and passersby began recognizing me and calling out, "VIC-tor! VIC-tor! VIC-tor!" The juxtaposition was jarring, unforgettable, and more than a little bizarre. I'd be lying if I didn't add that it was also a great feeling.

I was drawn back to Israel more than once, and I must say, the people were uniformly warm, friendly, and welcoming, with an inherent humanity I believe is the result of a lot of suffering. So it was horrifyingly unexpected one day when a driver picked me up at the King David Hotel, and about three or four hundred yards away there was a huge explosion, which turned out to be the bombing of a bus full of Israelis by a Palestinian extremist.

My immediate reaction was "Now I understand why the Israelis want to attack them!" and then, almost simultaneously, "What motivated the Palestinian to do such a thing?"

I was asked to go to the hospital to meet and comfort some of the victims. I did, and it filled me with rage on their behalf, until I caught myself and remembered that rage is what lies at the heart of the exact kind of violence I was witnessing.

Far greater minds than mine have tried and failed to solve these incredibly complex political and emotional issues, but it seems impossible not to think about them and ask questions, whether they're answerable or not.

I finally arrived back at the King David Hotel. I'd been invited by Malcolm Hoenlein, executive vice chairman of the Conference of Presidents of Major American Jewish Organizations, to attend a gathering in the hotel ballroom. I was in brilliant company, sitting beside Malcolm and sharing a table with the evening's keynote speaker, Princeton scholar and author Bernard Lewis, widely acclaimed as the most influential postwar historian of Islam and the Middle East.

After Lewis's speech, I seized the opportunity to have a conversation with him about the 1953 Iranian coup d'état in which Mohammad Mosaddegh, Iran's democratically elected prime minister, was overthrown in favor of Shah Mohammad Reza Shah Pahlavi—a coup orchestrated by the United States'

CIA and British intelligence for one reason and one reason only: oil. Mosaddegh demanded oil revenues, while the shah allowed unimpeded access to Iran's oil. It was yet another example of the West imposing our will against the Middle East, under the disingenuous guise of "spreading democracy."

On this same trip, I had the pleasure of playing tennis with Israeli tennis champion Amos Mansdorf, and of spending time with Mordechai Spiegler, who remains to this day Israel's record soccer goal scorer. He took me to see a team he managed, and we visited the Israeli parliament together. And I had lunch with an incredibly fascinating woman named Orna Porat.

Orna Porat was the first lady of Israeli theater, born Irene Klein to a Catholic father and a Protestant mother in Cologne, Germany. She joined the Hitler Youth during her high school years, and she became a stage actress in Schleswig during the war. She also began learning about the atrocities of the concentration camps and was subsequently interrogated by a British intelligence officer named Joseph Proter, who also happened to be a German Jew. This unlikely couple fell in love, married, and moved to Palestine, where she changed her name to Orna Porat, learned to speak Hebrew, converted to Judaism, and resumed her acting career. By the time I met her, she'd become an Israeli cultural icon, and I won't forget the stimulating two hours we spent together over lunch in Tel Aviv.

My abiding interest in Israel and its people culminated in a trip to its annual tourism conference with Prime Minister Ariel Sharon in 2004. It was at that conference that Yuval Rotem presented me with a humanitarian award from the Israeli government. I treasure the plaque, which reads, "With deep appreciation and gratitude for your warm friendship and your unwavering commitment to the state of Israel."

Several months later I traveled to Istanbul, Turkey, which was a whole other source of beautiful, historic fascination.

I stepped off the plane into the terminal to find large banks of lights and cameras and a crowd of veiled women shyly craning their necks in a cordoned-off area, and I tried to hurry along a bit to make way for whatever visiting dignitary had drawn such an enthusiastic crowd. When it became apparent that all this excitement was aimed at me, that those lights, cameras, and veiled women were there to witness the arrival of Victor Newman, I must admit my first thought was, "You must be kidding!" My second thought was, "I wish Bill and Lee Bell were here to see this." As overwhelmed as I was, I could only imagine the feeling of creating a television show that would cause this much hysteria halfway around the world.

My son, Christian, was with me on that trip, as were my *Y&R* colleagues and good friends Tracey Bregman and Ed and Melody Scott. We had bodyguards everywhere we went, and we were treated like royalty. I had a private meeting with Tansu Çiller, Turkey's first and only female prime minister. Ed Scott and I went for a run one day and came across a sandlot soccer game in progress, and the players were delighted when "VIC-tor" joined them. One night, Christian, Tracey, Ed, Melody, and I took a trip across the Bosphorus to a beautiful open-air café for a late-night dinner. There are times when the deep well of cynicism in me gives way to pure gratitude. That was one of those times.

I looked up my old childhood nemesis, Paul "Dickie" Johannsen, while I was there. He and I had outgrown our compulsion to beat the living shit out of each other the instant we made eye contact, and he was now a successful Bayer Pharmaceuticals executive, happily living with his wife in Istanbul. We played two hard sets of tennis one day, both of us refusing to let the other win, after which Paul gave me a lesson in the art of negotiating. It involved a combination of friendly enthusiasm and alcohol. His wife proceeded to tell me about a notoriously effective salesman at a carpet store in the middle of a famous Istanbul bazaar who'd purportedly mastered this particular art, and she issued a challenge.

"I'll bet if we take you there," she said, "you'll end up buying one of those rugs."

I assured her that I'd be damned if I was going to be manipulated into buying a rug from some slick, fast-talking Turkish carpet peddler, and off we went the next day to the bazaar.

It was extraordinary, to say the least—huge and crowded and colorful, full of energy, nonstop chatter, and the widest possible variety of wares for sale. Christian, his girlfriend, Paul, his wife, and I made our way into the carpet store, where we were greeted by the world's most enthusiastic salesman, who claimed to have the exact item I was looking for. (Interesting, I thought, since I wasn't looking for anything and was only there for the purpose of saying no and walking out without buying a thing to prove a point.)

He disappeared for a moment and returned with a rolled-up rug, handing me a snifter of brandy before unfurling the rug at my feet and launching into a unique sales pitch:

"Imagine this in your home, with a beautiful young woman lying across it, waiting just for you . . ." he began.

I rolled my eyes, but I was listening.

Several narratives and two or three brandies later, I said, "I'll take it."

The rug is still in our house today.

I was being mercilessly teased by my shopping companions until we stepped out of the store into the vast expanse of the bazaar and discovered that word had spread about my presence there, as shopkeepers and customers alike greeted us with a loud chant of "VIC-tor! VIC-tor! VIC-tor!" It literally gave me goose bumps. I smiled, again picturing the looks on Bill and Lee Bell's faces if they could be there to see the impact of their creation on, of all places, a Turkish bazaar.

On a separate, unforgettable trip, Dale and I met Ed and Melody Thomas Scott in Italy, where I was presented with Italian television's highest honor by Italy's prime minister Silvio Berlusconi.

One of the many things I truly love about Italy is the nonchalance with which they approach time and scheduling. The awards gala was due to begin at eight thirty. It actually got under way at around ten. And while it was a lovely event, I must say, the real excitement for me happened afterward, when Berlusconi invited us to a five-star restaurant in Milan. In addition to being prime minister, he also happened to own A.C. Milan, one of Italy's most famous soccer clubs, and all of his players were there. I was a big fan of the team, so sharing a meal with them was an absolute pleasure.

As if he hadn't already been more than generous enough, Prime Minister Berlusconi subsequently invited Dale and me as his guests to Villa d'Este, a luxurious hotel overlooking Lake Como. Between the gardens, the flawless hospitality, the cuisine, the red clay tennis courts where I played with the local pro, and the magnificent suite where I did my daily push-ups and sit-ups and shadowboxing, we were completely spoiled by the time we left, and it more than made up for the hours of soccer talk Dale gracefully tolerated at that restaurant in Milan.

IN THE LATE FALL OF 1996, I WAS HONORED AT THE THIRTY-Eighth Monte Carlo Television Festival.

I'd been to Monaco a few times before and loved it. Wendell Niles, who'd defeated me at Ping-Pong at an Arthur Jacobs party, had invited Dale, Christian, his girlfriend, and me to a tennis tournament there a few years earlier. He put us up at the Hôtel de Paris, and we practiced on red clay courts at the Monte Carlo Country Club overlooking the Mediterranean. Wendell knew everyone, so it was no surprise to find ourselves surrounded by Harry Belafonte, Sean Connery, Roger Moore, Sharon Stone, Monica Seles, Indian tennis champions the Armitrage brothers, Bernie Kopell, and many, many others. It was a spectacular trip, topped off by dinner one night at a Greek restaurant, one of those places where you break all the plates once you've finished your meal. Everyone got very loaded—so loaded, in fact, that to this day I can't remember how or why I ended the evening riding a donkey.

I do remember Harry Belafonte approaching our table and asking if I'd mind coming to say hello to his dinner companions, who were big *Y&R* fans and wanted to meet me. I was happy to oblige, of course, and spent a pleasant few minutes shaking hands with Harry's friends. One of them, a distinguished older gentleman, was particularly effusive about meeting "Victor." When Harry escorted me back to our table he said, referring to the older gentleman, "Do you know who that was?"

I had no clue.

"That was Habib Bourguiba," he said. "The president of Tunisia."

The president of Tunisia. A *Y&R* fan. It was hard to wrap my head around it.

Several years later, the year I was being honored at the Monte Carlo Television Festival, Dale, Christian, and I decided to take the opportunity to rent a Mercedes and drive through Europe en route to Monaco. Not until we were on the road did we discover that a truck drivers' strike was making it necessary to circumvent France and travel through Switzerland instead.

Christian was driving as we inched our way along a serpentine alpine road in bumper-to-bumper traffic. We'd planned the trip to arrive just in time for the cocktail reception in Monte Carlo—in fact, Dale was already wearing her dress and stilettos—but we hadn't allowed for this delay, so we were already tense, trapped in this endless, ridiculous line of cars crawling along at no more than one or two miles per hour.

Then Dale announced with some urgency that she had to pee. I'm sure I didn't greet this news with appropriate compassion, but I opted to go with her. The car was virtually standing still, so we had no trouble hopping out and heading into the thick trees and foliage by the road, Dale carefully picking her way along in her highest dress heels in search of a discreet place to relieve herself without entertaining the steady stream of slowly passing motorists.

It seemed to take her forever. I was furious with her by the time she emerged from the trees, and she was furious with me for being furious with her. To compound the anger, we arrived back at the road to discover that Christian had continued with the flow of traffic and was now about a hundred yards away, headed up a hill. We hiked after him as quickly as Dale's high heels would allow, finally caught up with him, flung ourselves into the car, and began yelling at him for driving on without us. So now Dale and I were furious with each other, we were both furious with Christian, and he was furious with us for being furious with him—as he rhetorically asked at the time, what the hell else was he supposed to do when the traffic kept moving and there was no way for him to pull over?

It was the first time that we, as a family, had ever officially stopped speaking to each other. We drove along for a good two hours in total, tense silence, refusing even to look at each other.

Finally, still without a word, we stopped at an Italian restaurant along the way and, after several more minutes of silence at the table, suddenly burst into one of the longest bouts of hysterical laughter that we, as a family, had ever experienced.

Between there and Monte Carlo, we came across a pounding rainstorm, so we arrived at the reception very late and very drenched. And I must say, while I'm sure it was a world-class evening, I have no memory of the cocktail party, but I'll never forget the trip there, nor will my wife and son.

As always, the people of Monaco, including Prince Albert, Princess Stéphanie, and Princess Caroline, were perfect hosts, charming and hospitable. We stayed at the historic Hôtel Hermitage on the Mediterranean, home to Russian nobility after World War I, and we enjoyed Monte Carlo's storied casinos. There was a steady stream of red carpets and interviews and parties and dancing and, of course, my favorite part, the annual tennis tournament.

I was paired for the doubles final with Monaco's prince Albert, whom I knew to be a very talented player. I'd noticed early in our match that Prince Albert's tension level on the court seemed to increase when his father, Prince Rainier, arrived to watch the match—purely an observation, and none of my business, but when we found ourselves losing four games to one in the second of a three-set match, I couldn't resist turning to my teammate and saying, "Fuck it, Prince, let's go!"

He smiled, nodded, and echoed my words, and the change in him was instantaneous. He focused on the game again and loosened up to become the player I knew was in there somewhere.

And I'll be damned: we won.

Again, purely an observation, but when Prince Rainier presented us with our trophies at the awards ceremony, I sensed a coldness between him and his son. As a father, I couldn't imagine it, and I hope I was wrong.

Through these adventures and many more, I was always aware that all these five-star privileges and all this attention were due in large part to *The Young and the Restless* and Victor Newman. And without the countless fans I met along the way in every airport and city and country I visited, there would be no *Y&R* and no Victor Newman, and I could still be auditioning for guest-star bad-guy roles on other people's series.

I've seen celebrities treat fans like dirt, like utter inconveniences, and it disgusts me. I distance myself as quickly as possible and privately wish those celebrities a long, happy future in the fast-food industry. None of us are divinely entitled to fame and success, after all, and the very least we can do is be gracious to the people who could just as easily be turning their attention elsewhere.

I had two great teachers who exemplified the best of the best when it came to humble appreciation of their fans. Neither of them was aware they were teaching me anything. They were just being themselves. I just had the unforgettable experience of being there to witness it and learn from it.

One was Pelé, arguably the greatest soccer player in the history of the game.

The other was Muhammad Ali.

It was 1980. Pelé's team, the New York Cosmos, with my

countryman Franz Beckenbauer, were playing in Los Angeles, and a cocktail reception was being held for him at the Bistro in Beverly Hills. The who's who of Hollywood, from Sean Connery to Gregory Peck, was on hand, and I took Christian, age ten, who was more excited about seeing Pelé than he was about seeing any of the movie stars in the room.

Pelé arrived right on time, with that wide, friendly smile of his, nodded hello to everyone, and I'll never forget it, headed straight for the kitchen, where he took his time greeting and chatting with the busboys, the line cooks, the chef, the dishwashers, and every other behind-the-scenes restaurant employee. When he finally emerged he looked around the room, spotted Christian—i.e., the only child in the room—walked straight over, shook my son's hand, and posed for a picture with him.

Not until then did he start saying hello to the rest of the A-list guests, while I stood there marveling at him. It was as genuine, almost artful, as anything I've ever seen, and it made an indelible impression on me—there wasn't a person at the Bistro that night who didn't get a few minutes of Pelé's undivided attention, and I left that party admiring him even more than I had when we'd arrived.

I knew that Muhammad Ali was a fan of *The Young and the Restless,* and I had the pleasure of attending his fiftieth birthday party at the legendary Chasen's restaurant, again with Christian by my side. But I'd never spent any one-on-one time with him until I boarded a flight from Philadelphia to Los Angeles. I was about to take my seat when Ali's close friend and photographer

Howard Bingham came up to me and said, "If you wouldn't mind, the Champ would like to say hello."

If I wouldn't mind? Are you kidding me?

I ended up sitting with Muhammad Ali for the duration of that cross-country trip. We talked about boxing, of course, and *The Young and the Restless,* and he showed me some magic tricks. The five-hour flight seemed to take about thirty minutes.

What amazed me was our walk through LAX and the absolute awe Ali inspired in every person in that terminal. People of every nationality, every walk of life, and every age from eight to eighty stopped dead in their tracks to gape at him as if they suddenly found themselves in the presence of a god. Some of them summoned the courage to approach him, and those who did were treated with a charm, focus, and generosity that went far beyond obligatory courtesy. Rather than his fans making him feel important, he made each of them feel important. It was extraordinary, and an example I've strived to follow. If Muhammad Ali, the Greatest, one of the most recognizable celebrities in the world, could take a moment to extend himself to a stranger, who the hell are the rest of us to take the position that we can't be bothered?

Muhammad Ali passed away while I was writing this chapter.

Thank you and God bless you, Champ, for the decades of excitement, for the inspiration and example, for an unforgettable day of travel, and for shadow boxing with me in the elevator of the secret exit at LAX. There will never be another like you.

11

THE GOOD, THE BAD, AND THE MORTIFYING

It occurs to me from time to time that I've been playing Victor Newman on *The Young and the Restless* for almost half my life. It seems hard to believe, but it's true. Small wonder, then, I guess, that *Y&R* has been the source of many experiences to which I ascribe superlatives, both good and bad.

My worst day at work as an actor, for example, was the day of a very, very unfortunate altercation between me and Peter Bergman, who plays Jack Abbott, Victor Newman's long-standing enemy on the show. Peter had come to *The Young and the Restless* to replace the original Jack Abbott, Terry Lester, after a very successful run on *All My Children* in New York.

I signed a nondisclosure agreement, which precludes me

from going into any detail about the altercation. So you might be wondering why I'm bringing it up if I can't discuss it, especially since it happened so long ago, but there are actually a couple of reasons for that.

For one thing, it was highly publicized at the time, and very upsetting for a lot of people, and I don't want to create the impression that I'm deliberately and conveniently avoiding the subject. If I could talk about it, I would. Then again, if the executive I asked repeatedly that day to take care of it had done his job, I can assure you, there would be nothing to talk about, because it would never have happened to begin with.

For another thing, I do want to take this opportunity to emphasize that I have nothing but respect for Peter and for the importance of the Victor/Jack relationship on *Y&R*. I admire him as an actor and as an impeccable professional, and I thoroughly enjoy working with him.

No subtext, no "but," it's just as simple as that and always will be.

The most embarrassing moment of my career, without a doubt, came as a result of the death of the unparalleled creator and fearless leader/head writer of *The Young and the Restless,* Bill Bell, on April 29, 2005. Bill was appropriately honored with a tribute at the 2005 Daytime Emmy Awards.

I had the pleasure of copresenting the final award of the show that night, the Best Daytime Drama, with none other than the Queen of Soul herself, Aretha Franklin.

As you may or may not know, from the moment we presenters first set foot on the stage at the Daytime Emmys, the teleprompters begin flashing our names in rapid succession, not only to remind us whose line comes next but also to urge us to hurry the hell up, which is more annoying than words can possibly describe.

But that night, whether they liked it or not, I wasn't about to leave the stage without an ad-libbed personal acknowledgment of my late, great boss and friend. So when Aretha and I finished our brief, scripted introductory pleasantries, I leaned into the microphone and, intending to say something like "May I personally add, God bless Bill Bell," instead, thanks to my name flashing on that fucking teleprompter, came out with "May I personally add, God bless Eric Braeden."

The audience, of course, began laughing, during which I forced a chuckle and a weak "What a Freudian slip *that* was," and then proceeded to announce, "And the Emmy goes to . . ." until Aretha interrupted to remind me that we hadn't read the list of nominees yet.

The Emmy went to *General Hospital,* which mercifully shifted the focus to the applause and hysteria of executive producer Jill Farren Phelps and company making their way toward the stage.

To say I was mortified is an understatement, and never in my life have I been more grateful to leave a stage. I truly wished there had been a convenient hole to crawl into, and I swear to you, while I'm not sure if it's good news or bad news, I was sober as a judge that night.

To the surprise of absolutely no one, it was my dear colleague Jeanne Cooper who took the greatest delight in my televised embarrassment. In fact, she had a plan, I was told, to have T-shirts made for everyone in the cast with their names, preceded by the words "God bless"—"God bless Jeanne Cooper," "God bless Joshua Morrow," "God bless Melody Thomas Scott"—to be worn at the studio on a day when I'd be there. Thankfully some shiny object came along and distracted her before she got around to following through, although I must admit, it would have made me laugh.

There's really no competition for "most egregious castmate." That distinction was securely snared by an actor whose name I don't care to mention. Those of you who are fans of *The Young and the Restless* will know who I'm talking about. Those of you who aren't won't care. I also want to make it clear that what follows are my own recollections of my experiences with him. I'm sure he has his own version of these events.

According to popular opinion, I'm the bully who got him fired. I assure you, if I had that much power at *Y&R,* he wouldn't have lasted nearly as long as he did. He has no one to thank but himself for the fact that he lost a job at which he could have been enormously successful.

I was very impressed when he first arrived. He was a talented, interesting actor, and I told him so. He reciprocated, telling me how much he loved working with me. I actually looked forward to our many emotionally complicated scenes together.

So it was shocking to hear from friends on the crew that he was routinely asking behind my back, "How long do you think that old son of a bitch will be around before I take over?" I was further told that a network executive was encouraging an inflated sense of importance to the show, assuring him that they intended to develop his character to replace Victor Newman as the most powerful man in Genoa City. (I can only assume the executives think their conversations never work their way down to the sound-stage floor.)

I didn't think a whole lot about it the first time he parked in my clearly marked parking space. Parking is at a premium at CBS, and I worked hard for a lot of years to earn that reserved space, but mistakes happen. The second time it happened I asked him to kindly move his car and not park there again. It would have been easier to accept his apology if he hadn't followed it up with the excuse, "I didn't know you were working today." I pointed out that he should have known, since all his scenes that day involved his character and mine, on which he simply shrugged and walked away.

The third time, though, I was furious. Rather than run the risk of escalating this relatively trivial problem into a major confrontation, I simply went to one of our producers, filled him in, and said, "This is obviously deliberate now. Tell that asshole to knock it off."

Minutes later there was loud pounding on my dressing room door—it seems "that asshole" had heard me complaining to the producer and thought he was going to get in my face about it. Instead, I just yanked open my door, said, "Don't you ever bang on my door like that again, and stop parking in my parking space. You're fucking with the wrong guy," and slammed the door.

Before long, friends in the cast and crew were pulling me aside to warn me that he was now declaring to anyone who would stand still long enough to listen, "By the time I'm through with him [me] he will have lost his job, his car, his house, his family . . . I'm going to clean him out." I became convinced that he was trying to bait me into hitting him so he could, at the very least, sue me for assault. Tempting as it often was, I'd be damned if I was going to give him the satisfaction.

The closest I came was during rehearsal for a scene that involved several of us, including him and me, when he did one of the rudest things an actor can do to his scene partners—he pulled the director aside to quietly discuss the scene in private rather than include everyone in the conversation. I'd called him on it when he'd done it before, but that day he did it again anyway.

Cameras were rolling by the time I blew and yelled, "Haven't I asked you not to do that?"

He marched up to me, inches away, yelling back at me, so I dared him. "You want me to hit you? You hit me first. Go ahead, give me your best shot, you fucking coward."

I knew he wasn't about to take a swing at me. Instead, he

stormed away. And if he was looking for a lawsuit against me for assault, it was thwarted yet again.

And then there was the day I stepped out of my dressing room to find Michelle Stafford, who was playing Phyllis Abbott at the time, in the hallway with her adorable little girl, talking to the actor in question. Michelle called me over to introduce me to her daughter, whom I happily made a fuss over for a few minutes before heading on to the sound stage.

Imagine my outrage when later that day the actor went on Twitter to post, "Not all men with mustaches are pedophiles. But all men who are pedophiles have mustaches."

No, I still didn't punch him, but believe me, it took all the self-restraint I could muster, much as it did when he conspired with a castmate to very publicly undermine a story line of mine. Contrary to what may be popular belief, never in my life have I started a fight. I don't instigate, but I'll sure as hell react.

Other members of the cast and crew on *The Young and the Restless* had their own difficulties with him, from what I understand. There were publicized allegations of a problem with one of our younger actresses, for example, but I know nothing about that situation personally, so I can't speak to it.

By then, between television and film projects, I had around a hundred and twenty credits on my résumé, and to this day I've never worked with anyone more seemingly determined to blow what could have been a great opportunity. I was delighted to see him go, and I wasn't alone. But in spite of all that, people were saying *I'm* the bully who got him fired. I'll be damned if I'll take responsibility for that. I still say he has no one but himself to blame.

On his last day, he came to my dressing room. "Man," he said, "I just want to tell you I'm so sorry about [blah, blah, blah and whatever]."

I was completely honest with him. "Forget it. Don't worry about it. You need to see a shrink. You're a good actor, but you're also self-destructive."

And he was gone.

End of story.

If only for the entertainment of Doug Davidson and some of our senior crew members who were there at the time, I have to mention a *Y&R* director named Frank Pacelli, the least favorite director of my career.

Personally, there wasn't a sweeter man on this earth than Frank Pacelli, and I was enormously fond of him.

Professionally, when he put on his director's hat, he was a tyrant, a megalomaniac who had to have everything precisely his way to the point of absurdity. He had a podium on wheels, with a light and a cup holder and a slanted top to hold his script, and he would stand behind it giving directions like "On the third line in this speech, I want you to pick up your pencil and put it over here." Never a word about our performances, mind you, just "Cross your arms when you finish that first sentence." If we told him once we told him a thousand times, "Frank, just have the fucking cameras ready and we'll do what feels right, okay?" It always fell on deaf ears—he couldn't bear the thought of not having total control of things that couldn't have mattered less to begin with.

He drove everyone crazy. Doug Davidson, only half-kidding, I'm sure, wanted to beat him up, and when Doug Davidson, one of the most good-natured, easygoing actors on *Y&R,* wants to beat you up, you've gone *much* too far.

Even our stage manager, Don Jacobs, a man with the patience of a saint, was pushed over the edge one day when we were shooting scenes on Hope's farm. There was a chicken in the scene, and Frank kept yelling, "Cue the chicken! Cue the chicken!" Finally Don snapped and yelled back, "Frank, *you* cue the fucking chicken!"

I hadn't realized how close I was to the end of my rope until early one morning during blocking. I was grumpy and still in the process of waking up when, after taking my seat at Victor's desk as indicated in the script, Frank said, "Pick up your coffee cup when you finish your first line."

I walked straight over to him, grabbed his wheeled podium, and chased him around Stage 41 with it for a good five minutes, to the great hilarity of everyone who witnessed it.

It didn't change his approach to directing one bit, but it was gratifying as hell, and some of the crew are still chuckling about it twenty years later.

The awards that have come my way as a result of *Y&R* have

given me some of the most deeply touching moments of my career, no matter how blasé I might have appeared about them at the time. I observed to someone not long ago, when they asked if I was excited about a nice bit of news, "I'm quietly excited, but I've been around too long for euphoria." I'm sure I sometimes feel more gratitude than I show, and I'd like to rectify that for the record.

I was completely overwhelmed, as I mentioned earlier, to receive a star on the Hollywood Walk of Fame. Then the People's Choice Award for Favorite Actor in a Daytime Drama Series and the Emmy for Outstanding Lead Actor in a Daytime Drama Series came along, in the same year. I was enormously honored by both, but the People's Choice Award touched me more deeply than the Emmy, probably because it came from the fans. I was unable to attend the Daytime Emmy Awards that year, for reasons I'll explain in another chapter, but had I been there, I might still be standing onstage thanking people, despite the producers' infuriating practice of cutting off the winners' acceptance speeches in midsentence to make sure there's plenty of time for incomprehensible musical numbers and comedy routines.

On my twenty-fifth anniversary at *The Young and the Restless,* I was presented with a certificate from Los Angeles councilman Tom LaBonge, signed by L.A. mayor Antonio Villaraigosa, proclaiming my twenty-fifth anniversary on the show to be "Eric Braeden Day" in Los Angeles. The celebration seemed almost surreal—much like at the Walk of Fame ceremony. I'd catch myself looking around at my family and friends and castmates and thinking, "*Me?* Really?" CBS president Les Moonves spoke. Political commentator and talk-show host Bill Maher spoke. Former castmate, professional wrestler, and Minnesota governor Jesse Ventura spoke. My old friend Esther Williams spoke. Melody Thomas Scott, Eileen Davidson, Josh Morrow, and Jeanne Cooper spoke . . . and spoke . . . and spoke. It was a day far beyond anything I would have even presumed to imagine.

And now, for the amusement of castmates and fans and the probable exasperation of the executives, here are the most annoying, in my opinion, and most easily corrected aspects of *The Young and the Restless.* I've spoken up about the majority of them many times, to no avail, but rest assured, very often what bothers you bothers us too, and it never ceases to amaze us that you, our viewers, notice *everything*.

It's a constant source of irritation to me, for example, that Victor Newman's office seems to have become the Newman Enterprises break room. People endlessly stroll in and out, sometimes to confront Victor about something, sometimes to just hang out and talk among themselves whether Victor's there or not. It would appear that Victor, billionaire founder and head of the company, no longer has a secretary to announce people and give him the option of either seeing them or sending them away. But I'm trying to imagine taking it upon myself to amble into the office of CBS president Les Moonves, whether his secretary's there or not, to discuss something at my convenience, or saying to my coworkers, "Let's go have a chat in Les's office and, while we're at it, help ourselves to his private bar." It's preposterous, and it's detrimental to the powerful Victor Newman character Bill Bell created more than three decades ago. As much as any of us dislike admitting it, there really is such a thing as a social hierarchy, and breaching it, presumably for the sake of budget constraints or production convenience, seems both careless and lazy.

And speaking of strolling in uninvited and the irrefutable reality of a social hierarchy, let's talk about Victor's home, the Newman Ranch, for a moment. Occasionally an unwanted visitor rings the doorbell and Victor demands to know how they got past security. Apparently any idiot can get past security at the Newman Ranch, since anyone, everyone, and their grandmother often show up at the door whether they'd ever be welcome there or not, with no mention of security whatsoever. It's bad enough that the Newman Ranch, after Sharon went on a bipolar rampage and burned it down, looks exactly like a rest home in Reseda. Can't we at least agree that there either is or isn't a security team at the entrance to the mansion of a Genoa City billionaire who has plenty of enemies and then be consistent about it?

I know it's a soap convention, and soaps don't always aspire to a realistic depiction of human behavior, but I also find it ridiculous when a script calls for characters to talk out loud to themselves, either to reveal a plot point to the audience or to allow an eavesdropper to overhear information they're not supposed to have. Who the hell does that? Why not a simple voice-over instead?

And why not see to it that core characters have close friends in whom they can confide when the need arises? In his early years, Victor Newman had a best friend named Colonel Douglas Austin (played by a delightful English actor named Michael Evans), and Victor and Katherine Chancellor were great friends as well—there was nothing they couldn't tell each other, they understood each other and had each other's back, and they could call each other out on their bullshit when the need arose. Victor hasn't had a close friend since Katherine Chancellor's portrayer, Jeanne Cooper, passed away. I miss the facets of Victor that came out most often in scenes with her—his heart, his kindness, his sense of humor, his vulnerability, his ability to relax and be himself with no agendas and no need to be defensive.

It's also a source of regret to me that *The Young and the Restless* has just a shadow of its former global presence. I keep wondering if any efforts are being made to correct that. Whoever's job it is to try to sell "Daytime's #1 Drama" to overseas markets, my colleagues and I would love to be kept apprised.

I have no doubt that I'll always have complaints about *The Young and the Restless,* and I also have no doubt that I'll speak up about them. Sometimes loudly.

But in the end, I'm deeply grateful to have had Genoa City as my home base for the past thirty-seven years, even when other projects have come along and temporarily lured me away.

12

TITANIC AND *THE MAN WHO CAME BACK*

I've continued to do occasional feature films and television guest-starring roles since I started on *The Young and the Restless* when the scripts have appealed to me. The general change of scenery and characters can be stimulating. They also remind me what an extraordinary phenomenon our *Y&R* shooting schedule really is—when you're accustomed to filming between eighty and a hundred pages a day and suddenly find yourself on a movie or prime-time show that averages maybe ten or twelve pages a day, it almost feels like a paid vacation.

Two movies that dramatically stand out from the rest, though, felt like anything but paid vacations. One of them I had to be talked into against my will. The other I leaped into. And both of them, each in its own way, were invaluable, once-in-a-lifetime experiences.

TITANIC

I came very close, more than once, to turning down *Titanic*.

They were considering me for the role of John Jacob Astor. They sent the script, I read the scenes, and I immediately thought, "Why would I do this? There's nothing here! I'm supposed to audition to be a glorified extra?"

Dale and Christian teamed up against me and convinced me to at least pursue the role, if only for the opportunity to work with James Cameron, and since they've been known to be right more often than not, I agreed, with great reluctance, to go through the motions, if only to appease them.

My first meeting didn't exactly spark my enthusiasm.

I dutifully showed up at Warner Bros. to meet the casting director. My position was and is that if I can arrive on time after driving all the way across town, the casting director, who's presumably already there, can sure as hell be on time as well.

After five minutes in the reception area with no acknowledgment whatsoever, I asked the secretary if the casting director was even in her office.

"She's on the phone," she said, as if that should mollify me somehow.

"Get her off the phone," I said, "because I'm about to leave."

With that, the secretary disappeared into the inner office and reappeared a moment later to gesture me inside.

I walked into this bleak, empty room and stood at the desk of an ice-cold casting director who, I had the impression, resented her phone call being interrupted for something as trivial as being prompt and courteous.

"What are you doing here?" she asked.

I replied, "I'm asking myself that same question," and walked out.

That, I was sure, was the end of that, and good riddance.

A few weeks later they called my agent again, this time in a panic. "Oh, please, please, please have him come back. James Cameron wants him, blah, blah." After several more similar calls, and a repeated explanation that there was really nothing in the role to make it worth my while, I finally got tired of hearing about it, and of Dale still encouraging me not to pass this up. I agreed to go back for one more meeting, and *only* one more meeting, provided my agent would send me all the information he could find on John Jacob Astor.

I arrived early for that second meeting and sat in the parking lot skimming through the John Jacob Astor material. I'll be damned, he was actually an interesting man—German American, inventor, businessman, financier, helped build the Waldorf Astoria Hotel, a lieutenant colonel in the Spanish American War, the richest man on board the *Titanic*, traveling with his eighteen-year-old wife, Madeleine, who was a year younger than his son by his first wife, etc. I was marginally more enthusiastic this time as I entered the building.

The same casting director who'd seemed so dismissive the first time couldn't have been nicer and more prompt this time as she led me into the same empty office, which now included the added feature of a video camera.

She handed me the script and asked if I preferred to sit or stand for this audition.

"Just turn on the damned camera and tell me what you want me to do," I replied, straining for patience.

She showed me three or four lines. I read them on camera, and she thanked me, ready to excuse me.

I'd been there less than five minutes. I at least wanted my gas money's worth, so I said, "No, wait, let me tell you a little something about John Jacob Astor," and proceeded to regurgitate everything I'd just learned about him in the parking lot, if only to make her sit there and listen to it.

I got the part, on the condition that whenever I was needed on *The Young and the Restless,* I would come back from Mexico, where *Titanic* was being shot.

Dale and Christian were as happy about it as I wasn't.

Resigned, I settled into my seat on a plane from Los Angeles to San Diego one morning, pulled out the *Titanic* script, read it from beginning to end, reviewed the John Jacob Astor scenes two or three times and thought, "What the fuck am I doing?" I'd grown tired of doing thankless little guest-star parts decades ago, and this was different how, exactly?

The flight was delayed, and we were still sitting on the tarmac. I called the flight attendant and asked if I could please get off the plane.

"Unless it's an emergency, no," she said.

It was a close call, but I finally decided that "changed my mind" probably didn't qualify as an emergency and settled back into my seat, feeling as if there might as well be bars on the windows of that damned airplane.

A hippie-looking driver was waiting for me in the San Diego airport baggage claim area, holding a sign reading TITANIC. As we headed toward Tijuana, he casually asked, and I quote, "Are you looking forward to working with the big asshole?"

"What do you mean?"

"What a dick," he growled. "I can't stand him."

I was already depressed enough, and now this? Just what I needed, an asshole director to look forward to, for a role I had no business taking in the first place. Perfect. I fumed all the way to the hotel in Rosarita Beach.

Alone in my hotel room, I was seriously considering calling the same driver and asking him to take me back to the airport when he showed up to drive me to the set instead. Feeling more like a hostage than a member of the cast, I went along, on a drive through what I'll politely describe as some of the less scenic parts of Mexico, until we arrived at the beach and I found myself staring at the *Titanic* itself, or the one side of it Cameron and his crew had built, with sets constructed around and in front of it. Cameron, I was told, had made twelve dives to shoot footage of the actual wreck site on the floor of the Atlantic and worked from the *Titanic*'s original blueprints to re-create the ship, exteriors and interiors, identical to their original scale. It was stunning, I had to admit.

I was summoned to wardrobe, where I was handed various articles of period formal wear to try on. During this, a man who was helping me into a dinner jacket said, "So, are you ready to work with the biggest prick that ever was?"

Oh, for God's sake. "Are you serious?" I asked him.

"What a fucking asshole," was his reply, and my determination to get out of there and head home escalated exponentially. But before I could put an escape plan into action, an assistant arrived to ask, very politely, if I'd mind stopping by the set to say hello to the producers.

"Sure, why not?" I sighed.

The set really was one of the most extraordinary things I'd ever seen, and the producers couldn't have been more welcoming and congenial. We were exclaiming over the remarkable *Titanic* re-creation when a voice behind me interrupted with a friendly "I'm so glad you're here!"

It was James Cameron, hand extended to shake mine. He was extremely respectful and the polar opposite of the raging, egomaniacal tyrant I was expecting. I decided to stick around after all and see how this played out, although I still wondered why he'd thought of me for this part and how I'd been on his radar in the first place.

The answer came during filming. We were in the middle of a scene when all of a sudden Cameron turned to me and shouted, "Never!"

I had no idea what he was talking about and asked, "Never what?"

"You know"—he smiled—"the last line in *Colossus: The Forbin Project.*"

He was a *Colossus* fan. Mystery solved, and I was flattered.

It took me three months to complete the small role of John Jacob Astor on *Titanic,* not because of problems on the set but because, as agreed, my commitment to *Y&R* took precedence when there were scheduling conflicts. On more than one occasion I finished filming for the day on *Titanic* at ten or eleven at night, jumped into the car in Rosarita Beach, flew up the San Diego Freeway like a bat out of hell, and made it to the CBS sound stage in Hollywood in time for my seven A.M. call on *The Young and the Restless.* If it sounds like a grind, I assure you, it wasn't. I loved it.

While *Y&R* was on its Christmas break, I was given permission to bring my family to the *Titanic* set. The film was still shooting, but Cameron took the time to graciously invite Dale, Christian, and me into his trailer to show us the opening credits, scored with Celine Dion's "My Heart Will Go On." I got goose bumps from it. I told him he was going to make a fortune, and it was an easy prediction to make—you could feel every bit of the power and the passion of Cameron's commitment to that project in every frame of film from the very beginning.

Of course, the longer filming took and the further over budget it went, the more often the Paramount and Fox executives started showing up, concerned that what was becoming, at the time, the most expensive movie ever made would be a bust at the box office. Cameron wasn't about to pander to them. I happened to be standing behind him in the line at the craft services table one day when his assistant scurried up to say that the "suits" were waiting for him.

"Fuck 'em," he said. "I'm eating. I'll meet with them later onstage."

The executives' concerns were apparently not limited to the budget. They were concerned about the length of the film as well, for the usual noncreative, soul-crushing reason—the longer the film, the fewer the theatrical screenings, and the fewer the theatrical screenings, the lower the box-office profits. From what I was told, they wanted to do their own time-saving edit of *Titanic,* in response to which Cameron famously replied, "You want to cut my movie? You're going to have to fire me! You want to fire me? You're going to have to kill me!"

Variety columnist Army Archerd called me one day and asked how I thought *Titanic* was going. I told him I thought it was going to make a massive amount of money.

"Really?" he said. "You're the only person I've talked to who thinks so. Why do you say that?"

I replied simply, "It's a soap opera. A very expensive soap opera."

The concerns about the budget and the extended shooting schedule were palpable on the set, but there were no complaints and no way Cameron or anyone else was about to compromise the integrity of the project by trying to hurry things along. A lot of the crew wives who'd expected their husbands to be home weeks earlier started showing up at the Rosarita Beach set, and by all appearances, they passed the time watching *The Young and the Restless*. I can't begin to guess how many autographs I signed, and it was my pleasure.

If the brass balls with which Cameron approached anyone he perceived to be threatening the integrity of his film had translated to abuse of his crew, I would have found him offensive. I have a notoriously short fuse when it comes to directors being cruel to anyone on the set, from the crew to the cast to the extras to the stuntmen to the hair, makeup, and wardrobe people. From what I'd been told before I met him, I'd anticipated squaring off with Cameron before the shoot was over, but I can honestly say I never saw cruelty from him, not once. He knew more about every aspect of filmmaking than any of the various department heads, and I came away feeling I'd had the privilege of working with a genius. He and everyone else involved were nothing but professional and enjoyable every step of the way, on probably one of the most challenging films any of them had ever undertaken.

Billy Zane, Kathy Bates, Kate Winslet, every actor in that cast was extraordinary. And I must say, Leonardo DiCaprio does the most remarkable Jack Nicholson impression I've ever seen. I've rarely said this about anyone, but there's no doubt about it, he's a born actor. He reminded me of Brando, without a trace of self-consciousness, both on and off camera.

It was ironic, in a way, that a part I'd almost rejected because it seemed so small and insignificant ended up being the most terrifying experience of my career, compliments of the scene in which John Jacob Astor drowned on the Grand Staircase as the *Titanic* went down.

The Grand Staircase was constructed of solid oak on a steel-reinforced foundation. It was built slightly larger than its counterpart on the actual *Titanic* for a reason that exemplifies the incredible amount of thought that went into every detail of the movie—people in 1912, when the *Titanic* sank, were shorter than they are today, so the staircase was scaled up for the purpose of creating a more accurate proportion.

In this scene, John Jacob Astor would be on the Grand Staircase when a hundred and fifty gallons of water came crashing through the glass dome and filled the massive room with water from the floor to the ceiling. There would be twelve cameras on hand to cover every possible angle, operated by cameramen in diving suits, and obviously it had to be done in one and only one take.

They had a stunt double on hand for me, but the night before we shot the scene, the assistant director came to my hotel room and said, "James wondered if you'd be willing to do it yourself."

Never one to shy away from a challenge, I told him, "I'll do it, provided he'll let me have enough dry runs to feel it's safe."

We did dry run after dry run the next day, and thank God, because a few things went wrong every time. The nearby diver, on hand in case of an emergency, was mildly reassuring, the operative word being "mildly"—the truth is, I was more than a bit apprehensive. But finally I took a deep breath and said, "Okay, let's do this."

I started up the Grand Staircase. The cameras disappeared as the huge room filled with water that was getting higher and higher by the moment. And then, when my foot hit a certain step, the deluge came crashing through the glass dome, devouring everything in its path, completely consuming every square inch of the room and taking the life of John Jacob Astor. It felt like nothing short of a miracle that it didn't take mine too.

To everyone's surprise, including Cameron's, during filming the staircase itself broke free from its foundation and floated up to the ceiling. Cameron ultimately felt it probably lent an unplanned feeling of authenticity to the movie—apparently there's very little left of the Grand Staircase in the *Titanic* wreckage he explored and filmed, so it's probable that's exactly what happened when the actual ship sank.

I've never been more shaken and more relieved than I was

when that scene was over. I was told later than when Cameron watched the footage he was furious because the water hadn't exploded through the dome at the precise moment he wanted. I was grateful beyond words that we all knew there would be no "take two."

As of this writing, *Titanic* is the second-highest-grossing movie worldwide in film history, outearned only by James Cameron's *Avatar*. I'm not surprised. The man is brilliant, and he has my eternal gratitude and respect.

I'm man enough to say that Dale and Christian were right from the beginning, and my initial instincts were wrong.

I'm very glad I took that part.

THE MAN WHO CAME BACK

My friend Chuck Walker was the only white boxer on the 1976 Olympic boxing team, a team that included Sugar Ray Leonard and Leon Spinks. He also happens to be a fan of *The Young and the Restless*.

Chuck is from Conroe, Texas, near Houston. When he retired from boxing, he put together a production company in Conroe and made a series of smaller, low-budget independent films.

One day he asked me to read a script he'd written. He'd raised money to film it in Texas, and he wondered if I'd be interested.

It ultimately led to the most joyful experience of my career.

The original script was a revenge story set in the South in the nineteenth century. It intrigued me, but since I like films that have an historical context, I suggested we research that time in America and see if we could find a factual backdrop for it to keep it from becoming just another generic rage-and-retribution movie.

What we found was a violent labor strike that took place in 1887, during the post–Civil War Reconstruction era, which was a rich, important part of American history. The strike led to a tragedy called the Thibodaux massacre.

The massacre was ignited by a confrontation between Louisiana plantation owners, in concert with the state militia and a group of vigilantes, and the ostensibly freed slaves. Those slaves throughout the South had teamed up with the railroad workers to form a union ten thousand members strong, 90 percent of them black. The union demanded better working conditions and wages paid in real money rather than scrip—worthless money that was only accepted at the plantation owners' overpriced company stores, which created nothing more than a perpetuation of the slavery the Civil War had theoretically abolished. The plantation owners, with the support of Louisiana governor Samuel McEnery and state district Judge Taylor Beattie, both of whom also happened to be plantation owners, ignored the union's demands, and in the resulting confrontation approximately three hundred strikers were mowed down.

It was a gripping, historically accurate story, very much

worth telling as far as I was concerned, and a perfect context for Chuck's original idea, and I took both the script and its potential backdrop concept to a writer/director named Glen Pitre.

Born and raised in Louisiana, Pitre was a Harvard graduate who'd won any number of awards for his Cajun- and English-language films and was acclaimed as "a legendary American regional director." His film *Belizaire the Cajun,* starring Armand Assante, was screened at the Cannes Film Festival and gained international respect. Glen knew the culture and the history of the subject matter, and he knew how to write scripts that could be executed on a limited budget.

Glen did a rewrite of Chuck's script called *The Man Who Came Back,* and my interest in the project increased significantly. By now, I didn't just want to act in this film. I wanted to have the experience of producing it as well, having a hand in it from the ground up, from inception to completion. I wanted the responsibility of being the place where the buck stopped—whatever went right or wrong, the credit and the blame would be all mine. There would be no studio, no network, no politics, no corporate suits with no creative talent whatsoever looking over my shoulder, making arbitrary decisions by committee. I couldn't wait to get started.

We had a strong story and a strong script, which made it easy to put together the cast we wanted. George Kennedy, that gifted giant who played my father on *The Young and the Restless,* signed on immediately.

Armand Assante, star of Pitre's *Belizaire the Cajun,* said yes. Billy Zane, whom I'd worked with on *Titanic,* said yes. Carol Alt, a fellow celebrity driver at the Long Beach Grand Prix, said yes. Sean Young, whom I'd known for a few years, said yes. My longtime actor friend Peter Jason, the extraordinary James Patrick Stuart, my heavyweight champion boxer friend Ken Norton—it was "yes" after "yes" as an incredibly talented cast fell into place.

The one person I approached on *The Man Who Came Back* who turned me down was my son. By then he'd become a very skilled writer, and I loved the thought of working with him. I couldn't have respected him more, not for choosing to pass on the opportunity to direct this film but for the reason behind it—under no circumstance does he ever want there to be even a passing suggestion that he got any job because of me. From the beginning, he's insisted on earning his way into this business on his own merits, and he's doing exactly that, very successfully.

So Glen Pitre became both writer and director on *The Man Who Came Back,* and Christian was an enormous help behind the scenes, putting me in touch with his friend Stoeps Langensteiner, who was indispensable as both our director of photography and our camera operator, and with first-class postproduction people, including Clint Eastwood's editor, Joel Cox, who signed on and did a fantastic job.

The Man Who Came Back, again, inspired by the historic Thibodaux massacre, is set in Thibodauxville, Louisiana, in 1887, twenty-two years after the end of the Civil War. My character, Reese Paxton, had been a trained assassin in the Confederate army and is now a plantation overseer.

"Freed" slaves, who are still working in the sugarcane fields under deplorable conditions, finally go on strike to demand better treatment and reasonable pay in real money rather than scrip. The plantation owners initiate a vicious attack on the striking slaves to force them back to work.

Paxton steps up on behalf of his workers to demand justice. To retaliate, the town's powers that be drum up false charges against him, of which he's convicted and sent to prison. In the process, he's forced to watch the unspeakable execution of his family.

He's beaten and tortured in prison and ultimately escapes, a former trained assassin returning to Thibodauxville, *The Man Who Came Back,* to avenge the death of his family.

I took a couple of months off from *Y&R* for filming, all of which took place in Texas—some near Conroe; some in Brackettville on an old, meticulously preserved ranch where John Wayne shot *The Alamo;* and some on the Liendo plantation in Hempstead. It was a guerrilla-style shoot, no frills, no time to waste on self-absorbed diva bullshit.

Without dredging up irrelevant, long-forgotten details, I do want to say this for the record: Sean Young had a rather dicey reputation when she joined the cast. I sat her down before we started filming and made it clear that we were all counting on her to be disciplined and professional—we had all the budget challenges we could handle, and we literally couldn't afford anything less than impeccability from her.

Not only did she come through like a champion, but one of my fondest images from the shoot is George Kennedy, all eighty-three years, six-foot-four, three hundred pounds of him, sweating in that hot Texas sun between scenes with Sean sitting beside him every chance she got, so solicitous of him, kindly and patiently listening to all his stories of old Hollywood.

She made such an indelibly positive impression on me that when an appropriate role came along on *The Young and the Restless*—a character named Meggie who kept slipping alcohol into alcoholic Nikki's milk shakes as part of a plot to marry Victor and then kill him—I saw to it that Sean was cast in the role. Once again, she was a delight to work with and rose to the challenge of soap-opera acting with the utmost diligent skill.

In fact, beginning to end, there wasn't a single member of the cast and crew I would replace if we were starting over today. I couldn't have worked with a nicer, more professional group of people.

The cast and crew typically ate breakfast at the Conroe IHOP. Peter Jason and James Patrick Stuart were there one morning and realized they didn't have any money or plastic on them. What they did have were their paychecks, which the local bank refused to honor because the checks were issued in Los Angeles. Peter, never shy about raising his voice during a conflict, loudly announced, "We're here working with Victor Newman!" The bank promptly cashed their checks, and Peter and James headed back to IHOP. I ate there myself one morning, and by all accounts, the place was packed every day from then on until "Victor Newman" and the rest of the film crew headed back to L.A.

Like most independent films, despite every effort to cut corners wherever possible, *The Man Who Came Back* exceeded our budget. Investor Steve Bowen couldn't have been more of a gentleman about opening his wallet again, and I gladly invested a lot of my own money as well. We finished on time, more or less, and headed back to Los Angeles for postproduction.

I was pleasantly surprised at how interesting the work of postproduction was and how naturally it came to me. We actors pick up more than we think we do from spending day after day on the set, listening, watching, seeing the process of a show's evolution from film to air—the edits, the sound effects, the music, every bit of it matters, and every bit of it fascinated me.

I was particularly concerned about the music, which can go so right or so wrong when it comes to setting the tone of any production. We were fortunate enough to find composers Erik Janson and Phil Marshall to create the sound track for *The Man Who Came Back*. By no coincidence, I used to play soccer at UCLA with Phil's producer/director brother Frank Marshall, who cofounded the wildly successful Amblin Entertainment with his wife, Kathleen Kennedy, and director Steven Spielberg.

With Lionsgate Home Entertainment as our distributor, we premiered *The Man Who Came Back* on February 8, 2008, at the Aero Theatre on Montana Avenue in Santa Monica to a standing-room-only audience of castmates, friends, and the press. Dale and I gave a party at our house after the screening, and I must say, it was a magical night for me, celebrating a career dream come true surrounded by the amazingly talented team of professionals who made the whole experience a joy.

In the first couple of weeks after its release, *The Man Who Came Back* was the number one nontheatrical rental in America, and it stayed in the top ten of rent-to-own DVDs for several weeks. Amazing. Exactly what we'd all hoped, but amazing nonetheless.

I came away with only two regrets.

One was that, in an effort to depict the historically based events of the film as realistically as possible, I made it too graphic. It became apparent at the premiere that the violence overshadowed the story of *The Man Who Came Back,* and if I had it to do over again, I would certainly tone it down so that the audience wouldn't find it occasionally hard to watch.

The other was my realization that I should have become a director a long time ago. That is not to imply that I had a single complaint about Glen Pitre's work on *The Man Who Came Back,* believe me. I'm just talking in general about a skill I wish I'd learned. Directing is endlessly fascinating to me, and I think I would have been good at it. In fact, I'm convinced that if

I'd done a prime-time series instead of daytime, I would have started directing in my thirties or forties. I watch Martin Scorsese films and Clint Eastwood films and Michael Mann films and Woody Allen films not just with thorough enjoyment but almost as a student, reveling in the awareness that this is what directing looks like when it's done right. I admire my son's expertise as a writer/director enormously, and now that he's established himself on his own terms in this business, I won't be a bit surprised if I end up producing a project of his someday. I'll leave the directing to him, and to the other very talented directors I work with, but it will never stop me from silently wondering, "What if . . . ?"

13

BUT I DIGRESS

Meanwhile, back in my offscreen life, I'd never stopped enjoying speaking engagements, including several for a wonderful organization in Anaheim, California, called the Phoenix Club, founded in 1960 to preserve German culture, language, and customs. On October 10, 2000, I had the privilege of being asked to offer a few introductory comments for their upcoming keynote speaker and guest of honor, former Soviet secretary general and Nobel Peace Prize winner Mikhail Gorbachev. I wouldn't have missed it for anything.

In my opinion, Mikhail Gorbachev and President Ronald Reagan were the two most important men of the second half of the twentieth century—perhaps a surprising position, considering the fact that I'm a Democrat. But it was at their summit meeting in Reykjavic, Iceland, that those two visionary leaders discussed the elimination of ballistic missiles in their respective countries and the possibility of eliminating all nuclear weapons from this planet. I will always believe that their desire for *rapprochement* prevented a cataclysmic third world war. To be given the opportunity to personally thank Mr. Gorbachev not only for his contribution to the reunification of Germany but also for his obvious sense of global responsibility was humbling, to say the least, and I wanted to make sure that by the time I'd finished my remarks, everyone else in that room felt as grateful to him as I did.*

I took the opportunity that night to ask Gorbachev how close we'd really come to a nuclear conflagration.

His answer was a chilling "Very close."

He'd been prevailed upon by his generals to send tanks into East Germany, he told me. He'd refused, and that was the beginning of the demise of the Soviet bloc. It would probably have fallen apart on its own, he told me, because the Soviets realized they couldn't have kept up with America in the arms race. If not for Gorbachev defying his advisors and refusing to order an act of aggression against East Germany, the world could easily be a barren wasteland by now.

---

* *The speech in its entirety can be found in Appendix B.*

Unlike my meeting with Gorbachev, my introduction to Ronald Reagan came about quite unexpectedly. I won a celebrity tennis tournament at the Riviera Country Club that happened to be sponsored by President and Mrs. Reagan, and while accepting a trophy and a commemorative watch, I said a few words of gratitude to Reagan for his involvement in Germany's reunification. Nancy remembered this and invited me to give a similar speech at a fund-raiser at the Beverly Wilshire Hotel for the Reagans and the Kitchen Cabinet. It was an interesting evening—me, a Democrat, surrounded by a roomful of Republicans—but it wasn't an event about party politics, and regardless of some of his other policies with which I decidedly disagreed, my respect for Reagan's contribution to world peace was absolutely heartfelt. And it was a pleasant surprise to learn from some of the Kitchen Cabinet wives that Nancy Reagan was a fan of *The Young and the Restless*.

I was subsequently invited to a Reagan event at the Beverly Hilton, where I intended to be equally nonpartisan, conciliatory, and well behaved. But when I found myself sitting at dinner next to sports columnist Jim Murray, I couldn't resist bringing up a long-standing pet peeve of mine.

"I love your columns," I told him, very sincerely. "But I wish that you, as an intelligent, responsible journalist, would disabuse yourself of the notion that only Russian and Eastern European athletes use steroids and other performance-enhancing drugs in explosive sports. It's a one-sided, unfair, ill-informed position."

He was very interested, not at all defensive, and asked me to elaborate.

"It seems that every time the Russians or Eastern Europeans beat Americans at track and field, you invariably suggest that it's due to steroid and HGH [human growth hormone] abuse. There's no question that they use them, but there's also no question that performance-enhancing drugs are just as prevalent among American and West German athletes. Isn't it time for some honest, balanced journalism about that?"

This led to a fascinating conversation on a subject about which I, as an athlete and the father of an athlete, happen to feel very strongly. I have good reason to believe that the use of performance-enhancing drugs started in America, as far back as the 1968 Olympics. In fact, this same sentiment was very articulately expressed in an August 4, 2016, *New York Times* article by Michael Powell, titled "Lest We Forget, the U.S., Too, Spent Time in the Doping Wilderness." So, in a spirit of fairness, should we rescind every world record and every gold medal in all the Olympic games since 1968?

I think the same mistake is being made in the area of performance-enhancing drugs in sports as is often made in politics—an effort to solve a complex problem with a simplistic solution. It's lazy, it's arbitrary, it's facile, and it's invariably detrimental in the long run.

It's easy for a parent, for example, to think, "I would *never* give my son or daughter steroids or HGH." But let's say you're a parent in a blue-collar household, living paycheck to paycheck, with a son or daughter who happens to be a good student and a gifted athlete, and you know that a performance-enhancing drug could elevate your child's chances of getting an athletic scholarship to a top-ten university you could never afford without it. Would you still be so quick to say "never"?

Please don't misunderstand—I don't advocate the use of steroids and HGH. What I do advocate is a whole lot more medical and scientific exploration of the subject in general so that instead of arbitrary testing and across-the-board bans, there are educated rules and limits in place. Why not insist that the powers that be in professional sports, in Olympic competition, in high-stakes athletics in general, come to the table armed with proven facts about what dosage of performance-enhancing drugs is actually beneficial and what dosage is potentially harmful? Or, to put it another way, why not expect as much of those in charge as we expect of our athletes?

For the record, I've never taken steroids or HGH, nor has Christian. Then again, I was fortunate enough to be able to afford to send him to UCLA without having to rely on help from a scholarship, so I didn't have to face the decision I know a lot of people confront. In fact, I can honestly say I tried drugs of any kind only once in my life, and once was enough.

It was the early 1970s, and some friends invited me over to their apartment one night after a soccer game. We drank a little, and then out came a joint and a small gold flask of cocaine. My friends seemed to enjoy it, and I was curious, so hell, yes, let's see what all the fuss is about. I gave them both a try, and they certainly lived up, or down, to their reputation of being mind-altering.

I remember indulging in an insatiable need to pontificate about Sigmund Freud and Carl Jung. I believed every word that came out of my mouth was brilliant, and I couldn't get enough of myself.

I remember dizziness setting in when the older woman to whom I was pontificating launched into a long-winded response.

I remember a friend walking me downstairs to the street at about two A.M. He asked if I was all right. I replied, "Hell, yes," and began shadow boxing while he walked away.

I remember walking home in some sort of inexplicable zigzag pattern that made complete sense to me at the time.

I remember wanting very much to go to bed but finding it impossible to calm down enough to accomplish it for a good twenty minutes or so.

Most of all, I'm happy to say, I remember hating everything about how it felt to be on a drug high and never wanting to experience it again.

Yet another reason I'm so passionate about sports—a good boxing workout or weight-lifting session is a far better high than drugs could ever hope to offer, and I consider that preference a blessing.

I also consider it a blessing that I've been given many opportunities to express my political opinions on national television, whether or not the subject matter had anything to do with German-American relations. I particularly enjoyed my several appearances on Bill Maher's show *Politically Incorrect* and being a guest on Joe Scarborough's *Scarborough Country*. The topics were always varied, relevant, and stimulating.

My invitation to *Scarborough Country*, for example, came shortly before the Iraq invasion, and I remember pointing out that it was futile to discuss whether or not we should invade Iraq, because that decision had already been made.

"But," I said, "George W. Bush had better commit to at least ten to fifteen years of total occupation, accompanied by a total, nationwide demilitarization."

So, of course, the Bush administration orchestrated a brief stay in Iraq instead, de-Baathified Hussein's army, the Sunnis, installed a Shiite government, and created an immediate terrorist potential of angry Sunni soldiers who now constitute the core of ISIS.

I also remember suggesting to Bill Maher that President Bill Clinton's only impeachable offense was using a Cuban cigar.

And yes, in case you're wondering, I do occasionally regret not going into politics.

But I digress.

I'm suddenly reminded of my old friend and co-star Jeanne Cooper, who could cover more seemingly disparate topics in a ten-minute monologue than anyone else in the history of humankind.

I believe the subject at hand was my admiration for Gorbachev and Reagan and their profound impact on the ban of nuclear weapons and the reunification of Germany.

My outspoken passion for the integrity of my homeland and my countrymen didn't fall on deaf ears, as it turned out.

Not once but twice I was presented with the Bundesverdienstkreuz, the German Federal Medal of Honor. The first was given to me by Ambassador Ruhfus at the German consulate in Los Angeles. I received the second at Villa Aurora, a magnificent, historic residential gathering place in Pacific Palisades for German émigrés, artists, writers, filmmakers and intellectuals. I was overwhelmed, standing there accepting that award, imagining both times that somewhere, somehow, my parents were watching in proud amazement.

I traveled to Germany, where I was given a reception at the city hall in Hamburg and was asked to sign a ceremonial registry of visiting dignitaries called the Golden Book. I was also invited to the town square of Bredenbek, my hometown, to be officially declared an honorary citizen. I looked forward to it, and I appreciated it, but I was surprised at how profoundly shaken I was by it.

It had been several years since I'd been back for any length of time, and I was flooded with such a rush of unexpected feelings—a deep, almost aching reminder of my roots, my childhood, the boy I was, riding his bike on those roads, working on those farms, playing hockey with his brothers on those frozen ponds, forever losing a part of his heart and his innocence when he lost his father . . . a disquieting awareness of my own mortality, the stark inevitability of it, and with it an unexpected grieving for wasted time, unexpressed gratitude, the arrogance of taking it for granted that I'll wake up tomorrow . . . and the realization that despite all my travels, despite my great fondness for living in Los Angeles and America, and despite my success, there always has been and always will be a sad, quiet homesickness in me for a place that still exists but a place I know I could never be content to live in again.

But I'm not sure I've ever been quite as moved, to the point of tears more than once, as I was by my invitation to participate in the annual March of the Living, in which twenty thousand Christians and Jews from around the world gathered in Poland on Holocaust Memorial Day to visit the concentration camps, honor the millions who died in them, and celebrate the survivors and the triumph of the global Jewish community despite the Nazis' unspeakable efforts to eliminate them.

I spent the first night at a hotel in Kraków, an absolutely beautiful city, untouched by war, and spent the evening with a group of American Jews gazing out over a magnificent square.

A waiter took our drink order. Out of sheer force of habit, I ordered Russian vodka. The waiter gave me a look that transcended all language barriers and brought me Polish vodka instead.

In sharp contrast, the next night there was a huge gathering at the center of the Kraków ghetto. A plaque on a small remaining section of the ghetto's former walls reads, "Here they lived, suffered and perished at the hands of Hitler's executioners. From here they began their final journey to the death camps." We all sat in the open air, on grounds from which thousands upon thousands of innocents were sent off to be exterminated at nearby Auschwitz-Birkenau, and I don't have words to describe the feeling of being there as a German, silently promising yet again never to stop trying to atone in every way possible for the sins of the fathers.

Abraham Foxman, director of the Anti-Defamation League and a Holocaust survivor, gave a very moving speech. "Let us not forget," he said, "that the only European countries who stood by us, who refused to cooperate with the Nazis in rounding up Jews, were Bulgaria and Albania." And indeed, it's very much worth remembering how rampant anti-Semitism really was then, and what a horrifying danger it turned out to be.

The next day we were taken by bus to Auschwitz, where it's thought more than a million Jews were annihilated. The crowd was massive as we marched from Auschwitz to the death camp, aware with every step that we were walking the same path along which all those innocent men, women, and children were led to the gas chambers. The barbed-wire fences, the fortified walls, the gallows, the gas chambers, the barracks, the row of chimneys marking the crematorium where all those starved, tortured bodies were burned, the railroad tracks leading into the entrance on which trains delivered throngs of helpless prisoners to be annihilated . . .

There aren't words.

It broke the heart and chilled the soul.

Tears in our eyes, we all gathered in a huge seating area in front of a massive crematorium. I was sitting with a group of Israelis and American Jews, and I'll never forget the utterly bizarre experience of several Israelis handing me their cell phones, asking me to say hello to their mothers.

And then came one of the most extraordinary moments of my life. I had no reason to believe that Foxman knew who I was, nor did I expect him to. But suddenly, after Ariel Sharon had been seated, Foxman was standing beside me, asking me to join him in lighting the ceremonial fire in front of the crematorium, in memory of all who survived. I was too moved and too humbled to express myself adequately at the time, but I will always hope he knows how very deeply grateful I am that he allowed me, a member of the German post-war generation, to share that once-in-a-lifetime honor with him.

Another honor I won't forget was being instrumental in bringing the Berliner Ensemble to UCLA's Freud Playhouse for their final appearance on an international stage on July 3, 1999.

They gave a brilliant performance of Bertolt Brecht's *The Resistible Rise of Arturo Ui,* with German actor Martin Wuttke starring in the title role. There were supertitles in English to the left and right of the stage, which allowed the celebrity-studded sold-out audience to thoroughly enjoy a German playwright's satirical, critical approach to the darkest period in German history. It was a thrilling evening, and it culminated in a party at my house that went on until four A.M.

It also brought back memories of many long-ago conversations I had with Tony Bates, our English Maccabees coach. He kept encouraging me to move to London to study and pursue my passion for William Shakespeare, and I kept reminding him that I was broke.

"You can make some money playing second-division soccer over there," he told me, and I can't begin to tell you how tempted I was and how seriously I considered it.

Looking back, I'm obviously glad I didn't go through with it. But I did start seeking out opportunities to perform Shakespeare here in Los Angeles and found my way into the L.A. Free Shakespeare troupe.

We performed *Macbeth* at several venues, with me in the role of Macduff, the archetypal avenging hero of the play. We used real swords onstage, which required a certain heightened vigilance—the sword tips kept breaking off in midduel and whizzing past my head, and I consider it a testament to my reflexes that I had the same number of ears when our run of *Macbeth* ended as I did when we started.

One particularly memorable night we were rehearsing in the band shell of MacArthur Park for our opening there the next evening. At around one A.M., a handful of people began wandering in and taking their seats in front of the stage. It was such a pleasant surprise. Los Angeles is not notoriously a "theater town" in general, and I remember thinking, "Wow, these people must really be interested in Shakespeare, to come watch a rehearsal at this hour! How wonderful!"

During a break, I was standing offstage when one of the Shakespeare enthusiasts tapped me on the shoulder. I turned to him, fully prepared for a brief, spirited conversation about *Macbeth,* or perhaps a compliment or two about my interpretation of Macduff.

Instead I was greeted with a weary "When are you assholes going to get the fuck out of here so we can get some sleep?"

It still makes me laugh.

I love Shakespeare, and I love a challenge, so I came up with a perfect way to combine the two—with the encouragement and guidance of Professor Cornelius Schnauber and the brilliant Louis Fantasia, I created a one-man show for myself, a performance of fourteen monologues from nine different Shakespearean plays.

On the one hand, it was a joy to study and memorize those monologues. The language is so extraordinarily beautiful and so profound that it's impossible to get tired of it or bored with it, and there's such perfection in it that you don't want to misspeak a single syllable.

On the other hand, I honestly thought I was going to lose

my mind preparing for opening night. Fourteen monologues written by almost anyone is a lot to memorize. Fourteen monologues written by Shakespeare borders on insanity. For weeks I'd wake up at two or three A.M. and stumble around the house quietly reciting a monologue or two and, half asleep, realize I'd mixed up *Richard III* with *Macbeth* or *Hamlet,* fall back into bed exhausted, and be too worried about it to fall asleep again.

When I wasn't worried about turning an evening of exquisite monologues into a random medley of Shakespeare's greatest hits, I worried about "going up," i.e., having a sudden lapse of memory in mid-monologue. When you "go up" doing Shakespeare, there's no panic quite like it, and there's no going back. It's not as if you can ad lib your way through until you're on track again, really nothing at all you can do but stand there in deathly silence, dimly hoping it looks as if you're simply taking a dramatically meaningful pause.

And then there's that other perpetual worry—it's surprisingly easy to get so caught up in the beauty of Shakespeare's words that you almost forget to perform them, so you end up simply reciting them instead and failing miserably to do them justice.

All of which is to say that on opening night, knowing the Verdi Ristorante in Santa Monica was filled with family and friends, I sat in my dressing room feeling as if my head was going to explode and wondering what on earth possessed me to think this was a good idea in the first place. As the stage manager counted me down—thirty minutes, twenty minutes, ten minutes—I felt that same urge to bolt and run that I felt opening night on Broadway so many years ago. But finally, as so many stage actors will confirm, with just a few short minutes to go, you finally reach a point where you think, "Fuck it. If I fall on my ass, I fall on my ass," and all you can do is walk onstage knowing you've prepared as best you can and hope for the best.

Thankfully, after all that worrying, it went very well. I'm not sure I've ever felt such relief in my life as I did when it was over . . . and of course, the minute it was over I couldn't wait to do it again. I wish I could do it again now. As I mentioned earlier, I had the pleasure of performing Shakespeare at the Wallis Annenberg Center for the Performing Arts in April of 2016 with my old friend Stacy Keach, Michael York, and several others, and I'll continue to participate in other Shakespeare tributes at every opportunity, but those only induce nervousness, not the preshow panic of carrying the evening all by myself.

I did my one-man show at several different venues over the years, including an especially memorable one at the Goethe Institute in Los Angeles, where I selected fewer monologues and performed them in both English and German. This commitment in L.A. is what kept me from being in New York to personally accept my Outstanding Lead Actor award at the 1998 Daytime Emmys.

So, if you'll forgive my tardiness, I'd like to properly thank the Academy and my *Y&R* colleagues in my own way, without the infuriating brevity dictated by the producers of the televised Daytime Emmy Awards.

14

THANK YOU, *Y&R*

As I write this, *The Young and the Restless* has just celebrated its 11,000th episode. It's obviously an amazing accomplishment for so many people. Understandably, it triggered an enormous amount of warm, grateful nostalgia in me as our cast, crew, writers, and network executives gathered to applaud ourselves and each other, not only for our 11,000 episodes but also for our almost thirty years as the number one daytime drama in television.

The presence of the late Bill Bell was pervasive. He was so brilliant at creating and writing in this genre that it's impossible to come up with adjectives about him that haven't already been overused. He was fiercely protective and independent when it came to *Y&R*—he wasn't about to tolerate interference from the suits or allow decisions about his show to be made by committee. He wrote one-year story arcs for his core characters, so we actors were never asked to deal with haphazard stories and characters that hadn't been thoroughly thought out. And if a story line wasn't working, Bill didn't equivocate, he just got rid of it in the blink of an eye. (One of the more classic examples was a character I can't recall, in the 1980s, who went upstairs to wash her hair and was simply never seen or heard from again.) He was a remarkable combination of uncompromising and responsive, sometimes refusing to budge on the wording of a line of dialogue, but also going above and beyond when I asked for a backstory for Victor Newman that would elevate him from cartoon to relatable human being. I'm proud to have known Bill Bell as a boss and a friend.

During the week of 11,000-episode celebrations, a sweet cameo scene was appropriately created for Lee Phillip Bell, Bill's widow and co-creator of *The Young and the Restless*. Lee is a lady, in the most classic sense of the word. I sometimes have trouble looking at her because I'm almost moved to tears by her grace and dignity and completely authentic charm, and by the amazing era she represents that so many of us will never forget. It's no surprise that she was a very popular talk-show host in Chicago for many years—she's an educated, articulate woman with a rare gift for forfeiting the spotlight to whomever she's talking to in even the most casual conversation.

Sharing that cameo scene with Lee was her and Bill's real-life daughter Lauralee Bell, who's been my castmate since the early 1980s in the role of Christine "Cricket" Blair Williams. I couldn't be more fond of Lauralee or admire her more. She could so easily have grown up spoiled and entitled, but not for one moment have I ever seen her take advantage of her position as "the bosses' daughter." Instead, she's a gracious, unassuming, hardworking, respected colleague, and I love working with her.

Another of our celebration episodes featured a wonderful montage honoring the late, great Katherine Chancellor and her beloved portrayer Jeanne Cooper. It's impossible to be at the studio without remembering and missing her—there are photos and cutouts of her everywhere, and rarely a week goes by when the cast and crew don't share a good laugh over one of thousands of Jeanne Cooper quotes and stories. What a piece of work she was, full of fire, kindness, orneriness, and laughter. Our scenes together as Victor and Katherine, who were close friends and confidants, were always an adventure. She never knew what might come out of my mouth, and I never knew what might come out of hers. What we did know, always, was that we cherished our relationship, both on camera and off. I have such a deep, abiding fondness and respect for her. She was a force of nature who survived this business for so many years as a single mother, who won her very public battle against alcoholism and illness, and, no matter what, still arrived at the studio four or five days a week knowing her lines and ready to work. Incredibly, she stayed on top of her game to the very end, right through what not even she knew would be the last scene of her career and her amazing, tireless life. I had the honor of speaking at the memorial service at Jeanne's home a few weeks after she died, and it's still difficult to believe she's gone.

Without a doubt the most enduring relationship on *The Young and the Restless* is the relationship between "supercouple" Victor and Nikki Newman. They've been married to each other, and to other people, more times than Melody Thomas Scott and I can begin to remember, and we've been asked in countless interviews what it is about Victor and Nikki as a couple that seems to captivate the audience. Without a doubt, as far as I'm concerned, a great deal of the attraction has to do with the fact that there's an equally enduring relationship between Melody and me. We "get" each other, and have from the very beginning, when Victor first laid eyes on a young, irresistible stripper named Nikki Reed. Our approach to work is so vastly different that it's almost hard to believe how compatible we are—Mel is very literal and likes to have lines and motivation and subtext explained, while I just want to get on with it and "shoot this shit." She's so talented and generous and so good at what she does, and there are few things I look forward to more than fight scenes between Victor and Nikki, after which it's not uncommon for us, as actors, to hug and say, "Good God, I love fighting with you!" But as well as we fight together on-screen, to the best of my recollection we've only had one offscreen fight in all these years, and I honestly can't even remember what it was about. It might surprise people to hear that Mel and I know very little about each other's personal lives. There's an unspoken agreement between us to keep it that way for at least another thirty-seven years so that we can sustain the deep, uncomplicated, mutual affection between us that undoubtedly translates to the screen. Maybe that's why, more than three and a half decades after our very first day of work together, we've never grown tired of each other and don't imagine we ever will.

The elder of Victor and Nikki's children, Victoria Newman, aged with remarkable speed and arrived at *The Young and the Restless* in 1990, in the form of a spectacular fifteen-year-old actress named Heather Tom. I adored her from the moment we were introduced on her first day on the set, and I always will. From the very beginning she was so bright and so talented, with an extraordinary work ethic. I was proud to attend Heather's high school graduation, and Mel and I watched in amazement as she was accepted to one Ivy League college after another but chose to stay in Los Angeles, continue working, and take UCLA extension courses instead. I was not a happy man when she left the show after thirteen years, but she's gone on to be a great success on our sister show, *The Bold and the Beautiful,* and by all accounts, an even greater success as a wife and mother. She has a special place in my heart.

It's no secret that I dislike change, and I couldn't imagine who could possibly replace Heather Tom as Victoria Newman. The answer turned out to be an actress named Amelia Heinle, previously on *All My Children,* I was told, and in no time at all I adored her too. She's smart, she's funny, she's sweet, she's focused, she's gifted, and she's a complete professional. There's a very special authenticity about her both on-screen and off and a natural vulnerability that makes it especially easy to play scenes in which it breaks Victor's heart when he and his daughter are angry with each other.

The same is true with Victor and Nikki's son Nicholas, played by Joshua Morrow. My least favorite scenes are those in which Nicholas is angry with or disappointed in his father and we have to be cold to each other. It's not easy to be cold toward Joshua, since offscreen he's a delight, personally and professionally. He and I share a preference for keeping it loose on the set, and after twenty-two years of working together, there's a lot of trust and comfort between us. I admire Joshua as a wonderful, devoted father and a sports enthusiast, and I'm so appreciative of his dedication to *Y&R*. I believe if he chose to pursue it, he could have a very successful prime-time career, but he's content right where he is, which isn't all that common a sentiment among daytime actors.

Melissa Ordway plays Victor's daughter Abby, the result of the theft of Victor's sperm by Abby's mother Ashley, and I must say, I couldn't be more fond of Melissa or enjoy working with her more. I've never seen a dishonest moment from her either in front of the camera or behind the scenes. She lights up every room she walks into without ever trying to be the center of attention. A few months ago I traveled to New York with Melissa, Christian LeBlanc (Michael Baldwin), Melissa Claire Egan (Chelsea Newman), Joshua Morrow (Nicholas Newman), and Sean Carrigan (Dr. Ben Rayburn) on a *Y&R* personal appearance tour and had a wonderful time. I already knew how much I enjoy working with these people, but they're every bit as engaging off camera, funny and unassuming and so generous with the fans, and of course, with Sean Carrigan being a former professional boxer, he and I are never at a loss for things to talk about.

Adam Newman, Victor's son by Hope Adams (Signy Coleman), the beautiful, blind farm woman Victor met and fell in love with in Kansas, was most recently played by Justin Hartley, who was a breath of fresh air from the moment he arrived on the set. He was respectful, professional, collaborative, and a damned good actor, and I thoroughly enjoyed working with him through the emotionally complex relationship between Victor and Adam. Like everyone else on the show, I was happy for him and not remotely surprised when he was lured away from *Y&R* by an NBC prime-time show called *This Is Us*. Justin has now left *The Young and the Restless*, prompting the death of Adam Newman in an explosion. Of course, Adam has "died" before, and I have no idea whether or not the character will resurface someday. But prime-time's gain is our loss when it comes to Justin Hartley, and I wish him the considerable success he deserves.

Robert Adamson plays Victor's grandson Noah, Nicholas and Sharon's son. He couldn't be a nicer young man. He also happens to be a very good actor whom I would like to see back on *Y&R* on a more regular basis, since I think both he and the character of Noah have a great deal of untapped potential.

Victor Newman's granddaughter Summer, Nicholas's daughter by his then-wife Phyllis (Gina Tognoni), has captured a piece of my heart, thanks to her remarkable portrayer Hunter King. What a pleasure she is. I always look forward to our scenes together and am perpetually impressed by how poised, engaged, and unspoiled she is and how thoroughly professional, especially for someone so young. The fondness with which Victor so openly regards Summer is an absolute reflection of my fondness for Hunter and her contribution to our cast.

I'm sure it's apparent on-screen how thoroughly I enjoy my scenes with Victor's youngest grandchildren Faith (Aly Lind), Connor (Gunner and Ryder Gadbois), Johnny (Holden and Ryan Hare), and Katie (Sienna Mercuri). (For die-hard fans with good memories, Johnny isn't technically related to Victor—he was the result of an affair between Billy Abbott and Chelsea Lawson while Billy was married to Victor's daughter Victoria. Victoria legally adopted Johnny when she and Billy reconciled.) They're all adorable, delightful little scene-stealers, and they bring out a softer, more playful side of Victor I wish were written more often.

Eileen Davidson joined *The Young and the Restless* in 1982 as

Ashley Abbott, Victor's occasional love interest and wife. Eileen and I are not close, and we've had a skirmish or two offscreen. But I have enormous affection for the Victor/Ashley history and wish it were written and referred to more often. One of my all-time favorite story lines was when Victor was alone, angry and grief-stricken after the sudden death of yet another of his wives, Sabrina (Raya Meddine). He left Genoa City and was hiding out in a monastery in Paris, back in the days when we actually went on location, and Ashley came to find him. The scenes were unforgettable, and the backdrop of that spectacular city only heightened the dramatic, romantic magnetism that has always existed between those two characters.

Many years ago Victor Newman had a brief affair with Jill Abbott, played by the remarkable Jess Walton. Jill was convinced that Victor was planning to marry her, and she didn't take it well when she learned that he had no such intention. Since then Jess and I have had very few opportunities to work together, but I'm an unabashed fan of hers, particularly in her most recent story line in which she's making aggressive efforts to keep her son Billy (Jason Thompson) away from his brother's wife Phyllis (Gina Tognoni), with whom he had an affair, and maneuver him back into the arms of Victor's daughter Victoria (Amelia Heinle), where she's convinced he belongs. (Victor, by the way, loathes Billy and couldn't disagree more vehemently.) It's exciting and energizing to have Jess back on the show after some extended absences, and to watch her commanding, fearless work.

It also bears repeating how strongly I feel that the historic enmity between Victor Newman and Jack Abbott is one of the most essentially interesting, complex dynamics on *The Young and the Restless* and how fortunate I am to be paired with Peter Bergman for that relationship. He is without a doubt the most disciplined, prepared actor I've ever known, and I couldn't be happier that we've come to respect and adjust to our vastly different approaches to our work.

Doug Davidson (Paul Williams) and Kristoff St. John (Neil Winters) are probably my two closest friends in the cast, and I couldn't admire them more as actors and as men. My only complaints about them are that Kristoff and I have far too few scenes together, and that Doug and I can barely look at each other when we share scenes because we're likely at any moment to burst into an uncontrollable fit of laughter in the middle of angrily yelling at each other.

I have that same spontaneous laughter problem with two other actors in particular, by the way—Christian LeBlanc, aka Victor Newman's attorney Michael Baldwin, and Ray Wise, who plays the nefarious former cult leader Ian Ward. They're both terrific actors who also happen to be terrifically funny, and it's all we can do to get through scenes together with a straight face. I'm hoping the writers will somehow mend the relationship between Michael and Victor that was ruptured when Michael was supposedly representing Victor in court but deliberately blew Victor's defense on behalf of his best friend.

Phyliss and Victor ended up in prison. As for Ray, while I wish him a long future on *The Young and the Restless*, I'm privately keeping an eye out for other projects we might work on together as well.

I admittedly don't watch *Y&R* on a regular basis, but when I do, I'm so impressed with our incredibly talented cast in general. I rarely share story lines with many of them and only see them at the studio between scenes. But it's no surprise to me, just from viewing occasional air shows, that we've been the number one daytime drama for all these years with, in addition to the many I've already mentioned, actors like Greg Rikaart, Beth Maitland, Daniel Goddard, Camryn Grimes, Bryton James, Jerry Douglas, Tracey Bregman, Jason Thompson, Steve Burton, Elizabeth Hendrickson, Gina Tognoni, and Christel Khalil on board.

Of course, a few very talented actors have left us over the years for one reason or another. Billy Miller, Michelle Stafford, and Victoria Rowell in particular come to mind. Two of them have been effectively recast, but I hated to see each of them go.

Shortly after the airing of our 11,000th episode it was announced that *The Young and the Restless* has hired a new head writer and a new story consultant. As much as I usually hate change, I'm feeling very optimistic about this one.

Our new head writer is Sally Sussman, whose first of many tenures with *Y&R* was in the mid-1980s. She worked side by side with Bill Bell and was part of the writing team that elevated us to the top of the daytime drama ratings, where we've remained since 1988. Sally knows this show as well as any of us do, and her loyalty to it and its legacy characters runs as deep as it does in our new story consultant, Kay Alden.

Kay started on *The Young and the Restless* as a script writer in 1974, a year after its television debut. She was indispensable to Bill Bell as he developed the show and some of its characters and ultimately became our head writer when declining health forced Bill to step down in the late 1990s. She left us about ten years ago, and we're all excited that she's back.

I've always thought, and I always will think, that head writers have the hardest job in show business. They're the first to get the blame from their cast and fans when story lines seem to fall flat and the last to get credit when things are going well. Bill Bell; Kay Alden; Jack Smith; Lynn Latham; Maria Bell; Josh Griffith; Jean Passanante and Shelly Altman; Chuck Pratt, and Sally Sussman should all qualify for hazard pay as far as I'm concerned, as should our script editor Brent Boyd, who's invariably the first person I call when I have what I'll politely call "inquiries" about a scene and/or story line. Our producer Tony Morina (who happens to be married to our new head writer Sally Sussman), former executive producer Jill Farren Phelps, and her successor Mal Young set themselves apart by always being present, available, and responsive to the cast, which is a rare and much appreciated gift.

I haven't always been able to say this, but I enjoy going to work these days, and a great deal of the credit for that goes to a crew for whom I have the utmost respect. They really are the true unsung heroes of *The Young and the Restless*. There are too many to mention them all by name, but makeup artists Patti Denney and Robert Bolger, who've seen it all, heard it all, and are still, thank God, the soul of discretion; stage managers Tom McDermott, Herbie Weaver, and the intrepid Don Jacobs, who lost his hearing from decades of getting yelled at from the booth; technical director Tracy Lawrence, production mixer Tommy Persson, and boom operator Mark Mooney, who've been with us forever and know all the stories; camera operators Kai Kim, John Bromberek and Luis "Chico" Godinez; Jennifer Johns, our former wardrobe mistress, with whom I had many a spirited political discussion; current director Sally McDonald and my old friend and director Mike Denney, who left us a few years ago but whom I still call from time to time because I miss him . . . Again, too many to name here, but to every one of them I'd like to say, "What a luxury to have the best crew in the business and step onstage day after day knowing that you have our backs."

And I must say, I'm deeply appreciative of the support and receptiveness of CBS Chairman of the Board, Chief Executive Officer and President Les Moonves. Les has always been a strong, loyal ally, and I feel a personal affinity for him, and pride in his remarkable accomplishments, because he started out as an actor. CBS is television's most-watched network under his leadership, which, in an industry as competitive as ours, is nothing short of incredible, and all of us at CBS, daytime and prime time, owe him our thanks.

I hate clichés, but sometimes they're too appropriate to avoid: All of us are most deeply grateful to the fans of *The Young and the Restless*. You're the ones who keep this show alive, keep a whole lot of good, hard-working people steadily employed, and motivate us to not let you down. And you satisfied a long-standing career goal of mine that I mentioned many chapters ago—since the day I became an actor, I wanted to be involved in a project that matters. Thanks to you, that's exactly what I'm doing.

15

IN CLOSING . . .

It's overwhelming at the age of seventy-five to take on the challenge of committing my life to paper and to do it honestly, for better or worse. One of my first thoughts when I began to even consider such a thing was "My granddaughters will be reading this." I imagine there are passages that will make them laugh and others that will make them cringe. In the end, though, it's my hope that they'll come away knowing that their grandfather always tried hard, worked hard, did the best I could with what I was given, and have loved them with all my heart from the moment they took their first breath.

I've never been one to second-guess my past circumstances and my decisions along the way. It seems like an exercise in futility to wonder about things I can't begin to revisit and change.

It inevitably just brings me back to the same bottom line: it was what it was, and it is what it is.

Mine is an unlikely success story. I sit here in the comfortable living room of Dale's and my home on a private cul-de-sac in Los Angeles, looking out at our spacious backyard splashed with the colors of Dale's beautiful, lovingly tended flowers, and even though I lived it all, I still wonder how I got here from the decimated, bombed-out German farmland where my brothers and I worked and played and presumably thought that was what the whole world looked like.

How can I begin to imagine what my life would have been like if I hadn't lost my father when I was so young? When you're twelve years old, your heroes are supposed to be invincible, immortal. I'm sure his death, and the suddenness of it, lies behind this spark of rage in me, and created the protective shell that I carry with me to this day—the message seemed to be that at any moment, from out of nowhere, unimaginable pain can be inflicted on you, and there's not a damned thing you can do about it, so you'd better keep your fists up, ready to fight, ready to defend yourself and those you love. It never made me a bully. In fact, I loathe bullies. But it did make me combative to this day when I feel I'm under attack.

Falling from financial security into poverty in the wake of losing my father instilled an inability to be complacent and an abiding cynicism from learning that "Just because you have it today doesn't mean you'll have it tomorrow." There's nothing ennobling about being poor. It's dehumanizing. It's hard to focus on academics when most of your time and energy are consumed by basic survival. I've always been blessed with an intense intellectual curiosity and the mental acuity to put it to good use, but formal education is a luxury until and unless you're not preoccupied with securing food, clothing, and shelter. I hear people say, "My parents put me through college," and I think to myself, "I hope you know how lucky you are." Even though I was never able to afford a college degree, I've always been and still am a voracious reader, never tiring of keeping my mind stimulated and educating myself on subjects that interest me, particularly world politics, world history, philosophy, and, of course, sports.

I shudder to think what might have become of me if it hadn't been for sports, and for the athletic talent I was given. Sports were a much-needed, productive outlet for all that rage and combativeness of my youth, and a much-needed area in which I discovered I could excel with a lot of discipline and hard work. They taught me the values of sportsmanship and teamwork and fairness and respect and playing by the rules. They provided me with a partial scholarship at the University of Montana. They opened more doors for me than I can possibly count and broadened my circle of friends around the world in incalculable ways. They gave me the stage on which I got to experience the art of losing gracefully and, incredibly, what it feels like to be a champion, and they gave me an invaluable gift to pass along to my son, who, thank God, shares my passion.

Somehow, against a lot of odds, and despite the hurt boy who will always be an underlying part of me, I came out of all that a happy man. I'll be damned.

I came out strong. I came out self-reliant. I came out empathetic and vigilantly protective of the underdog and those who've been hurt. I came out appreciative of everything I have, knowing I earned every bit of it. I came out fearless and outspoken, with an ironclad work ethic, a profound conscience, and yes, even a sense of humor.

I made it from the despair of Hitler's Germany to meeting and having meaningful conversations with some of the world's most important leaders.

I've met and, in some cases, formed friendships with some of the world's greatest athletes.

I've done all I know to do to advance German-Jewish dialogue and to put an end to the collective German condemnation that crystallized for me in 1961, wanting to shout out to the world and to the media, "I understand your rage, but when the hell will you finally start looking at us Germans as human beings again?" Sometimes I look back and wonder if I was just tilting at windmills, but I don't regret a moment of it.

With nothing but a great love of words and a lot of on-the-job training, I've been a successful actor for more than half a century in a business in which less than 1 percent of the membership of the Screen Actors Guild are able to earn a living as actors. I've worked with some of the most brilliant actors, writers, and directors in the industry and had the extraordinary experience of producing a feature film.

My passion for politics has led people to ask if I've ever considered becoming a politician. I'm self-aware enough to know that I don't have the temperament for it. NRA lobbyists and proponents of deregulation, for example, would not enjoy having me around, nor would those who've long since stopped thinking for themselves on the issues at hand and forgotten that compromise, seeing both sides rather than just the self-interested side of one party or another, is the essence of democracy.

I would never rule out the possibility of producing again, under the right circumstances, or of more Shakespeare performances, or of saying yes to other extracurricular roles, depending on the script and on who's involved. I might even take up golf someday . . . it's just that, as I delight in telling my golf enthusiast friends, I'm not old enough yet.

For now, I intend to keep right on doing what I'm already doing—

* staying very active;
* doing my daily workout routine;
* boxing and playing tennis several times a week;
* having breakfast every morning at the same unobtrusive café, often with my good friend Paul Brooks, sitting in the corner reading the *New York Times,* the *New York Review of Books,* and the German newspaper *Die Zeit;*

* enjoying frequent dinners with my son, my favorite companion in the world, talking about history, politics, sports, and scripts;
* being a good grandfather;
* being a good, loyal friend;
* calling my brothers—Horst, Peter, and Jochen in Germany—so often that if I added up my phone bills, I'd discover that I could probably have bought them all houses in my neighborhood by now;
* seizing every opportunity to travel to personal appearances;
* proudly going to work three or four days a week;
* and perhaps most of all . . .
* never letting a day go by when I don't take a moment to remember how blessed I am and say thank you.

An incalculable amount of my gratitude is reserved for Dale. If it weren't for her I would have left *The Young and the Restless* after three months. I wouldn't have changed my name and done *Colossus,* I wouldn't have done *Titanic* . . . I would have had an entirely different acting career, or perhaps no enduring acting career at all, out of sheer stubbornness, if it weren't for her instincts and her sage advice.

And of course it's Dale who's responsible for the greatest achievement of my life, my son, Christian Gudegast.

My son truly is my pride and my joy, my closest friend, and the finest man I've ever known, a fascinating blend of the best of his father and, thank God, the best of his mother. To add to the embarrassment of riches, he's given us three precious granddaughters whom we adore beyond all reason.

There's not an honor, an award, or a championship I've achieved in my lifetime that meant more to me than the note Christian enclosed in his Father's Day card to me this year:

> *I am very, very blessed to have you as a father. You have taught me everything—to be an athlete, honorable, generous.*
>
> *You taught me how to nourish the mind, to love reading and constantly learning.*
>
> *You taught me how to be charming and respectful of all men.*
>
> *You taught me how to be affectionate with my loved ones and how to be a loyal friend.*
>
> *You taught me discipline, how to live healthily, about nutrition and sports science.*
>
> *You showed me how to work hard and tirelessly.*
>
> *And most of all, you taught me how to be a badass motherfucker.*
>
> *You're the coolest dude I've ever known, Pops. You're a stud, and you are an undisputed success. Happy Father's Day.*

It took me years to finally commit to this memoir, vacillating between feeling I had a lot to say and wondering, "Who cares?"

In the end, I must say, I'm glad I did it, and I hope you've enjoyed reading it as much as I've enjoyed writing it.

Neither Victor Newman nor I is planning on going anywhere anytime soon, so by all means, stay tuned.

ACKNOWLEDGMENTS

With my sincere thanks to all those who participated in making this book a reality:

Dale Gudegast, Christian Gudegast, Lindsay Harrison, personal publicist Charles Sherman, Kathleen Tanji, Lesley Bohm, Sanjay Patel, Heather Leigh Jackson, Kathy Hutchins, and, at HarperCollins, Lisa Sharkey, Amy Bendell, Alieza Schvimer, agent Jennifer DeChiara, Victor Hendrickson, Jennifer Teng, Stephanie Vallejo, interior designer Renata De Oliveira, cover designer Ploy Siripant, publisher Lynn Grady, HarperCollins publicist Maureen Cole, and marketing director Michael Barrs.

APPENDIX A

THOUGHTS ON BEING GERMAN

FIRST DELIVERED IN SAN FRANCISCO FOLLOWING THE FALL OF THE BERLIN WALL

When I was accepting the invitation to speak at this banquet, I began to ponder anew the question What is it like to be German, or German American? How do I define my Germanness? In personal terms, I have early memories of bombings and fires, of having to be carried frantically into a basement, of the fear that gripped everyone at the sound of approaching Allied bomber squadrons that would inevitably unleash their destructive fury on cities and villages like mine, only to leave burning farms and screaming animals in flames in their wake.

I have memories of being hoisted onto the shoulders of my teenage brother so that I could see the city of Hamburg aflame after one of those devastating firebombings that left the city an inferno in which tens of thousands of civilians perished in one night.

I have memories of thousands of homeless and hungry people descending like desperate vultures, from devastated cities like Hamburg and Kiel, onto the countryside to frantically dig for any leftover potatoes or kernels of wheat.

I have memories of the Christmas Eve when my brother and I had to recite poetry to the local Santa Claus and sing "O Tannenbaum" and "Stille Nacht, Heilige Nacht," and only then could we turn to our presents, a pair of shoes perhaps, which would have to last until next Christmas.

I have memories of impromptu ice hockey games on frozen ponds and soccer games with pig bladders because we could not afford a real ball. Memories of a beloved father and hard school benches, of teachers who had come back from the Russian front with no legs and one arm, and great bitterness.

Memories of long hiking excursions on hot summer days, singing "Mein Vater war ein Wandersmann und mir liegt's auch im Blut," of secret rendezvous and adolescent kisses with my first love, Rosely, on country lanes. Of my mother saying, "Das koennen wir uns nicht leisten," when my brother and I were coveting a pair of soccer shoes in the store window. Oh, when I think of my hardworking, proud mother and father, who experienced the two most cataclysmic and devastating wars in the history of mankind, and who each time had to start over with nothing.

I remember *Tanzschule,* waltzing and doing the tango, and Elvis Presley, and Louis "Satchmo" Armstrong, and I remember leaving it all behind one day in May, when I was eighteen, while standing aboard the *Hanseatic* waving good-bye to my family while the orchestra was playing "Junge, Komm Bald Wieder."

I remember the first sighting of the Statue of Liberty, the skyline of New York City, the sweltering heat, the frenetic hustle and bustle of white- and black- and brown-skinned people, of taking the Greyhound bus through Southern cities, where they had separate toilets and drinking fountain for whites and blacks, and where a genteel Southern lady expressed her love for castles on the Rhine and *apfelstrudel,* and asked me what I thought of Hitler, and I said I didn't, and I hadn't.

I remember fulfilling my childhood dreams of being a cowboy when I was in Montana and going to university there, and being asked, one day in a lecture on philosophy, in front of the whole class, how it was possible that a country that had produced Goethe and Schiller and Beethoven and Schubert could produce Hitler and concentration camps. I was eighteen then and couldn't answer.

I remember the experience that left an indelible mark on my brain, and theretofore innocent German heart. It was in Los Angeles in a movie theater, where I saw a documentary called

Mein Kampf. I went to see it because its title promised something about Germany, and I was homesick. It showed scenes of concentration camps, goose-stepping soldiers, of Hitler kissing babies, corpses piled high in makeshift mass graves in concentration camps, of dead German soldiers standing frozen in the wind and the snow-swept steppes of Russia. It showed American soldiers liberating walking skeletons from camps.

It was then that I lost my innocence, and no one was there to explain or quiet my deeply felt sense of anger, betrayal, and shame. Had my beloved mother and father been a part of that?

They just could not have, and yet I remember sending letters filled with anger and bitterness and inexplicable disappointment to my mother.

I remember later playing for a Jewish team called the Maccabees. I fought hard for them, perhaps in the vain hope of atoning for the sins committed by some members of my parents' generation. I met Jews from Hamburg, a village in Hessen, from Cologne, Jews who had left in the thirties and who seemed more German in their old-fashioned ways and attitudes than I was. I met Jews who accepted me because I was too young, and Jews who did not accept me because I was German, and Jews who talked nostalgically of their favorite prewar soccer teams: Eintracht Frankfurt, or Dresden, or Hamburg, or reminisced bitterly about the insidious ways of anti-Semitism. I met Germans who called me a traitor because I played for a Jewish team, and I remember an Israeli teammate who talked like a racist about blacks and was suspicious of me because I was German.

I remember my first agent in Hollywood, a Jew, who was kindhearted and helpful, and gave me my first break in this tough business of acting. I recall Americans coming up to me when I played Captain Dietrich on *The Rat Patrol*, saying, "I wish you Germans had won the war, we wouldn't have to worry about the damn Russians."

I remember fighting with producers on how to play my role in *The Rat Patrol*. They wanted an eye patch and a limp in order to perpetuate the stereotypical image of a German soldier. I insisted on playing the Rommel-like figure as a human being with dignity because the German soldier of the Wehrmacht, who came back from the Russian front, was decent and brave and tough and fought for his country just like any other soldier. I remember a conversation I had with Curt Jürgens on the way to the theater in New York where I played his son in a Broadway play. He thought I should go back to Germany because in America I would play nothing but those damn Nazi roles, and I said it might take me a while, but I was determined to help destroy that caricature. I was determined to show that we were human beings with all the strengths and frailties, with all the feelings and thoughts, of any human being.

I remember my son coming home from grade school one day and telling me that he had been called a Nazi, and asking me what that meant. I remember my trying to explain something I had taken years to study and understand to a little boy.

I remember reading William L. Shirer's *Rise and Fall of the Third Reich,* and Alan Bullock's *Study in Tyranny*, and Albert Speer's *Inside the Third Reich,* and the best book about that fateful period, Sebasian Haffner's *Anmerkungen zu Hitler (Anecdotes to Hitler).*

I remember Simon Wiesenthal, during an interview, saying that the actual perpetrators of atrocities numbered about a hundred thousand, and Henry Kissinger saying under no circumstances was the postwar German generation to be held responsible for Auschwitz. I remember my admiration and respect for the German National Soccer Team, playing the World Cup in Italy. And then we became world champions. It was almost all too good to be true. Then came some editorials in the newspapers about the renaissance of German power and the caricature of Helmut Kohl as the new Hitler, and the many scathing remarks made by the cheap English press and character assassination by Margaret Thatcher and her cabinet, all warning of German power while bemoaning the loss of their own.

As a German, I wanted to shout out to the world, "When will you ever stop talking about those damn twelve years? When will you ever give us credit for more than forty peaceful democratic years during which Germany has been an exemplary democracy, a loyal ally of the Western Alliance, an unwavering friend of both America and Israel, a patient initiator through its Ostpolitic with a Communist East, and a country that has opened its arms to more of the politically disenfranchised, the persecuted and hungry, than any other except perhaps America? When will you ever talk about and acknowledge the untold contributions made by German immigrants who toiled for you, America, as carpenters, farmers, mechanics, longshoremen, doctors and nurses, coal miners, machinists, lawyers, surgeons and generals, teachers and scientists? When?" I ask.

Well, it will happen when we German immigrants and Americans of German descent start talking about it, and when we start addressing the issues that concern us, when we open our hearts and extend our hands to each other and to those who were wronged by another generation, when we become aware of our profound contributions to the success in freedom and democracy that is America.

For that purpose, a few friends of mine and I have founded the German American Cultural Society of Los Angeles. We want to preserve the histories of German Americans and their immigrant ancestors—be they Catholic or Protestant or Jew.

Our formerly divided Germany will become one again. Let us not forget Reagan, Bush, Baker and Mitterand, Kohl and Genscher, Gorbachev and Shevardnadze, who made the seemingly impossible a reality, and the thousands of brave East Germans who courageously cried out for freedom.

Because of our historical legacy, we Germans have a profound responsibility to be tolerant of others and to cooperate as equal partners in this world of many peoples. Tonight, let us remember the many positive contributions the Germans have made to mankind.

What does it mean to be German? It means that we are part of a community of mankind with a specific and complex heritage, and I am proud of that heritage. Thank you.

APPENDIX B

THE GORBACHEV SPEECH

DELIVERED AT THE PHOENIX CLUB IN ANAHEIM, CALIFORNIA, ON OCTOBER 10, 2000

Dear Mr. Gorbachev and Mrs. Gorbachev, Deputy Consul General Beck and Mrs. Beck, President Kunkel and Mrs. Kunkel, ladies and gentlemen:

It is my pleasure, and I feel deeply honored, to have been asked to say a few words of introduction about this evening's keynote speaker and guest of honor. His courage and vision are directly and profoundly tied to our celebration of the tenth anniversary of German reunification.

In the last ten years, a formerly divided Germany has become an integral part of a progressively unified Europe; for the first time in modern history, Germany is at the center of a peaceful alliance. It has become the driving force of economic and political cooperation on the European continent. Its neighbors to the east are no longer poised to wait for its demise, but instead are eagerly inviting German assistance in economic, scientific, and technical terms.

No longer are mighty armies, with the most devastating arsenals the world has ever known, facing each other across an Iron Curtain that ran through our beloved Germany like a never-healing wound. The nightmare of a mutually assured total annihilation has given way to a lively exchange of ideas, and economic and technical interdependence. No longer is European soil the arena for the nuclear arms race, densely saturated with missiles of unimagined destructive force, nor are the world's oceans teeming with floating weapons so powerful their deployment would have ended civilization as we know it.

No longer do Germany and America, along with their NATO allies, face a Soviet Union that in the 1980s spent a disproportionate 25 to 30 percent of its gross national product on weapons of destruction, nearly six times as much as the U.S. and its NATO allies.

Germany in the last ten years has extended its helping hand to most of the satellite nations of the former Soviet empire. The demand for German language instruction in Eastern Europe has increased dramatically. Personal contact and visits among ordinary citizens—something completely unthinkable only twelve years ago—are now a commonplace occurrence. Free enterprise and budding democracy have increasingly replaced the iron grip of dismally inefficient, centrally controlled economies.

For the first time in over seventy years, it is now possible to visit the country whose people have suffered through centuries of unimaginable deprivation and hardship and yet have given birth to the genius of Tolstoy, Dostoyevsky, and Solzhenitsyn, and the music of Tchaikovsky, Borodin, and Rachmaninoff.

The fall of the Berlin Wall, the disappearance of the Iron Curtain, the free exchange of ideas and goods and people across heretofore hermetically sealed borders, all this is revolutionary, and was born of the efforts of many people, most notably former presidents Reagan and Bush, foreign secretaries Shultz and Baker and Shevardnadze, Chancellor Helmut Kohl, and Aussenminister Genscher.

But no one person was more responsible for the most profound change in the geopolitical landscape of the second half of this past century, more directly involved in initiating the deeply longed for thaw in the icy and potentially explosive relations between the two hostile superpowers, than this evening's guest of honor. At the risk of losing his own life, he perhaps spared the lives of hundreds of millions who would surely have perished had the insane arms race continued unabated.

It was his vision of democracy and openness, of glasnost

and perestroika, his dream of peace among former bitter enemies, that allows us tonight to celebrate the reunification of Germany. Let us say thank you to the steadfast loyalty of Presidents Reagan and Bush and the American people.

But none of their efforts alone would have made this the more peaceful world it has become in the last ten years without the enormous courage and deeply humane vision of one of this century's most brilliant and important statesmen. Whenever he sets foot on German soil, he is spontaneously welcomed with outpourings of the deepest warmth and affection and gratitude.

Ladies and gentlemen, please welcome the last secretary general of the former Soviet Union and now citizen of Russia and the world, Mr. Mikhail Gorbachev.

Q&A WITH ERIC BRAEDEN

What was it like to write a book?

It was a relatively painless process to write the book. I sat with Lindsay Harrison and we tape-recorded many conversations, which we then turned into this book. There were a few corrections to make here and there from what Lindsay wrote with me. But on the whole, it was painless.

What kind of response have you received since the book's publication?

Fans have told me that they were really touched by the book, especially hearing about the early part of my life. Fans who love *The Young and the Restless* know me from TV, but they are surprised to hear about my early childhood experiences.

When you were thinking back on your career while writing your memoir, was there a particular moment or experience that stood out?

I would have to say it happened on my first job ever in the film *Operation Eichmann.* I had been given a script, didn't know what to do with it, and was saved by a very observant and motherly script lady, who quickly discerned I did not know what I had to do in a scene with Werner Klemperer (Colonel Klink on *Hogan's Heroes*). She quietly rehearsed the scene with me without anyone noticing, and it came off very well.

Do you see any similarities between yourself and the character of Victor, who you play on TV every day?

As an actor you draw from your own emotional reservoir and vivid memories. I wouldn't want to have as tumultuous a life as Victor does. Nor am I as intensely interested in business as Victor, but I am interested in politics, history, and sports. Nor would I put up with some of the trials and tribulations Victor has with Nikki. But then the show is about drama and conflict.

You've played so many roles. Is there one in particular that stands out as having had a big influence on your career?

Some of my early theater roles obviously helped shape my career. I played the prince of Wales in a play by Jean-Paul Sartre called *Kean,* then I was in a Tennessee Williams play early on. But is there one particular role that really helped? They all helped along the way. Some episodes of *Gunsmoke* and *Mission:*

Impossible helped a great deal—they showed me in an entirely different light. Some of the early roles on *Combat!*, that series helped. Those three are sort of stepping-stones. The confluence of the right script, the right part, the resonance it had with the public—that is so rare and so fleeting and so unpredictable that the business is essentially the business of gamblers, on every level: producing, writing, directing, etc. But that is part of the fascination as well.

You've had an amazing career from the stage, to TV, to film. Which do you like most? Why?

I used to want to do Shakespeare the most. But being involved in the production side with *The Man Who Came Back* was the most wonderful experience, and I would gladly do it again. I loved it and had more fun on that film than anything I've ever done, largely because I was involved in the casting of it and then the editing of it later on.

Is there a role that you covet?

I don't think so. If I had to do it over again, in the mid-1960s I was about to go to England to do Shakespeare, and only Shakespeare for a while, because Shakespeare is so demanding on every level—emotionally, intellectually, physically, just so damn challenging. But I didn't do that.

The only things as an actor that I used to covet were to be in an Ingmar Bergman film or a Woody Allen film. I thought about that for a long time. But beyond that, not really. I'm very happy with what I'm doing now. It's a hell of a job. I get to exercise my craft almost every day. I get to play for almost one hundred million people in the world, in various languages, and sometimes I pause to remind myself how deeply satisfying that really is, and how rare it is to have that chance.

Do you have a favorite show you've seen?
Seinfeld is arguably the best show I've ever seen. It is the best ensemble piece I've ever seen and probably will ever see. The writing is brilliant. I watch it every night.

If one of your granddaughters came to you saying she wanted to be an actress, what would you say to her?
I would encourage it. The young actresses on our show are very adept. If they're guided by responsible people, responsible actors, they can succeed. From what I've seen it matters so much who teaches you. And yet, only one percent of the 150,000 registered actors in Hollywood make a living.

What is it like having your son follow in your footsteps?
I love it. I just absolutely love it. I played a cameo on his film *Den of Thieves,* which he wrote and directed. To watch him direct was just so interesting. He obviously also learned a lot from my telling him stories of how not to direct, what psychological approach is best. He proved very good at all aspects of making a film. I'm very proud of him.